PENGUIN BUSINESS
THE SINDHIS

MARK-ANTHONY FALZON is a social anthropologist. He is a professor at the University of Malta and a life member of Clare Hall, Cambridge. His books include *Cosmopolitan Connections* (Oxford, 2005), *Multi-Sited Ethnography* (Ashgate, 2009), *The Examined Life* (2019), *The University of Malta* (2020) and *Birds of Passage* (Berghahn, 2020).

GURCHARAN DAS is a world-renowned author, commentator and public intellectual. His bestselling books include *India Unbound, The Difficulty of Being Good* and *India Grows at Night*. His other literary works consist of a novel, *A Fine Family*, a book of essays, *The Elephant Paradigm*, and an anthology, *Three Plays*. A graduate of Harvard University, Das was CEO of Procter & Gamble, India, before he took early retirement to become a full-time writer. He lives in Delhi.

THE STORY OF INDIAN BUSINESS
Series Editor: Gurcharan Das

To the memory of my grandfather,
Joseph Borg Bonello (1921–2020)

THE SINDHIS

Selling Anything, Anywhere

MARK-ANTHONY FALZON

Introduction by
GURCHARAN DAS

BUSINESS

An imprint of Penguin Random House

PENGUIN BUSINESS

USA | Canada | UK | Ireland | Australia
New Zealand | India | South Africa | China

Penguin Business is part of the Penguin Random House group of companies
whose addresses can be found at global.penguinrandomhouse.com

Published by Penguin Random House India Pvt. Ltd
4th Floor, Capital Tower 1, MG Road,
Gurugram 122 002, Haryana, India

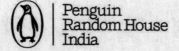

First published in Penguin Business by Penguin Random House India 2022

ISBN 9780143458388

Typeset in Aldine401 BT by MAP Systems, Bengaluru, India
Printed at Replika Press Pvt. Ltd, India

www.penguin.co.in

CONTENTS

Acknowledgements

The first phase of research for this book was carried out as part of my doctoral work in anthropology at Cambridge. My foremost words of thanks go to my supervisor, James Laidlaw, and my faculty advisor, Susan Bayly. Marilyn Strathern, then the head of department, taught us that renowned scholars can also be generous with their knowledge and encouragement. The Wenner-Gren Foundation and the Cambridge Commonwealth Trust provided me with the funds necessary to travel and do fieldwork. My college, Clare Hall, and later King's College, were generous with accommodation. The second, and recent, phase of fieldwork and writing was supported by the University of Malta. I am tremendously grateful to Gurcharan Das, the editor of this series, for entrusting me with this project, and for his advice. The Penguin team was patient and helpful throughout. The full list of Sindhis who helped me is too long, and I will limit myself to three recent names: Saaz Aggarwal, Nandu Asrani and Kavita Daswani.

Introduction

The secret sauce of Sindhi business success is made from the following four ingredients, according to Mark-Anthony Falzon: 1) the compulsion to strike out on one's own; 2) the will to succeed, surviving hard knocks and bouncing back after things go wrong; 3) the readiness to travel, move around and develop new markets; and 4) the knack of building a symbiotic web of family members and fellow Sindhis in distant places and tapping into this network when in need. These four qualities exist in some measure in all successful business communities. We have observed them in the three volumes published so far in this Penguin business history series about the Marwaris, Kachchis and Punjabi Khatris of Multan. We shall encounter them again in the forthcoming volumes on the Chettiars and Parsees. There is much in common between all business communities, but what uniquely differentiates the Sindhis is their global spread. Falzon has narrated many charming stories in this book to make his point. In the same spirit, let me narrate two personal experiences with two Sindhis—one a domestic story and the other international. Both throw some more light on Falzon's thesis.

The Magic of Ulhasnagar

There is a fourteen-foot-long horizontal painting by the Marxist urban landscape artist, Sudhir Patwardhan, that hangs in a dark passage in my house. Titled 'Ulhasnagar,' it has always conjured sad memories of my friend, Ramu Vaswani. Ramu's family fled Sind in 1948 with only the clothes on their back during the bloody Hindu-Muslim riots, when India was tragically divided. Ramu was a four-year-old refugee when his family reached Bombay (now Mumbai) by the sea before trudging 50 kilometres north to a refugee camp at Ulhasnagar in Thane district. He grew up in the mini-Sindh ghetto of displaced humanity amidst unbelievable suffering—no piped water, no electricity, no paved road. But Ramu willed himself to forget the trauma of Partition and went on to become an accountant. When I met him, he was doing the books at our company's auditors. Although he had risen in life, I'd always felt a little sad. The sorrow of his childhood memories of Ulhasnagar lingered in both our minds.

My perspective changed after reading Chapter 5 of this book. In it, Falzon reveals not the pain but the magic of Ulhasnagar. He narrates stories of hard work, self-reliance and enterprise—women preparing papads, achaars, embroidering clothes, which their men would hawk the next day on the suburban train to Mumbai. Soon, the family had saved enough to invest in a machine; before long, they built a successful, small business. By the late 1950s, Sindhis had bounced back. Ulhasnagar had become a hive of small-scale industry, its bazaars astir with shops and businesses. Falzon catalogues the sheer variety:

> There are, in fact, thousands of Sindhi-run businesses in Ulhasnagar. Many are small-scale: a printing press in a tiny room, a small warehouse for the wholesale of garments, and so on. Other Sindhis here may do subcontracting work for larger manufacturing companies: making a particular flavour for a biscuit brand, for example, or panel hinges for steel cupboards. The range of goods and materials produced here is mind-boggling and includes textiles, plastics, rubber, chemicals and paints, enamelled wares and electrical cables, pickles and spices, lighting and chokes, furniture, kerosene stoves, packaging materials, food products such as biscuits and bread, and pens and stationery. The goods and services traded include transport, car parts, textiles and jewellery.

It is true. Every Sindhi that Ramu introduced me to from Ulhasnagar had a rag-to-riches story to tell. The town is a testament to Montesquieu, the French eighteenth century Enlightenment thinker, who said that 'commerce is sweet'. He wrote that 'wherever the ways of man are gentle, there is commerce; and wherever there is commerce, the ways of men are gentle…the natural effect of commerce is to lead to peace.' The proponents of the 'sweet commerce' theory believed that the spread of trade and commerce would decrease violence and warfare among human beings. Trade civilized people, making them reasonable and prudent, more reliable, honest, thrifty, industrious and less given to damaging political and religious enthusiasm.

There is another side to Ulhasnagar, however, less sweet but more colourful. India's economy was closed in the decades after Independence and Indians hungered for foreign goods. Sindhis found the answer. They began producing jeans, shampoos, watches and handbags, labelling them proudly 'Made in USA'. It was just not the USA that people had expected; but it was USA, nonetheless—'Ulhasnagar Sindhi Association.' For years, Ulhasnagar became synonymous as the factory of fakes and counterfeits, giving my Marxists friends another reason to critique the 'sweet commerce' theory of free trade. Leftist never tired of reminding me that free trade was about colonial exploitation and slave trade, ranting on about 'commodification'—how the market makes people into commodities for exchange. They talked endlessly about ugly 'conspicuous consumption' by the middle class.

Leftists have a point. The 'sweet commerce' theory is both right and wrong. The impact of commerce, I have concluded, is both positive and negative. My feelings, as I look at my painting of Ulhasnagar anew, alternate between hope and a cautionary warning. The market both promotes and corrupts good morals.

Luckily, the main market for Ulhasnagar fakes happened to be next door in more tolerant Bombay, not Calcutta (now Kolkata), where Marxists were in power.

Bombay was born out of two words—sea and commerce. The sea came first. With the decline of the Mughal port of Surat in the eighteenth century, Bombay rose, thanks to its great natural harbour and miles and miles of deep, sheltered water, perfect for big steamships of the nineteenth century. This led to an explosion of commerce. It represented opportunity for someone like me 150 years later. Tall in the confidence of my 21 years, I came to live and work in Bombay in 1964, seeking fortune and adventure. I am typical of the millions of young men and women, migrants all, who come year after year seeking to make a life in India's premier commercial city.

It explains, why so many Sindhis made a soft landing here after the trauma of Partition. After losing their ancestral home in Sindh, they adopted Bombay, making it their 'cultural heartland'. They embraced the open city and it reciprocated by embracing them. Today, it is the Sindhi capital of the mind. David Copperfield in Charles Dickens's novel says of London, 'It is an "amazing place".' So is Mumbai (and Ulhasnagar.) Yes, it has slums like Dharavi. The movie, Slumdog Millionaire, showed us a humanity in the slum, teaching how a city grows organically. When people migrate from a village, they prefer a place where they are near their own, even though a slum. To service their needs, kirana shops, barbers, cycle repair and mobile phone recharging vendors pop up. The strength of Ulhasnagar and Dharavi are its face-to-face sociability, where street life is vital and where human bonds of inter-dependence are formed between strangers.

Interlude in Manaus

What makes Sindhis unique is their global spread.
Ulhasnagar is, thus, only one side of Sindhi story—a
purely domestic one, of being uprooted by Partition,
fleeing from Muslim Pakistan to the safety of India.
The Sindhi is also a global citizen. 'Is there any country
in the world that has no Sindhi in it?' goes the saying. I
discovered its truth in the heart of the Amazon jungle
in Brazil.

I happened to be visiting Rio on business and decided
to see the famous rain forest over the weekend. After a
sweating a whole day in the jungles, our boat docked
finally in Manaus, the main town of the state of Amazonas.
The desk clerk at the hotel was exceptionally solicitous
upon seeing my Indian passport. So, was the taxi driver
who took me to dinner at a restaurant nearby, where the
waiter was unusually polite, and so was the manager. Why
was I getting the red-carpet treatment? The answer came
a few minutes later, when a when a tall, sun-burnt Sindhi
walked in. He came directly to my table, asking if he
could join me. He was starved of company from home, he
confessed. Not only did he own the restaurant, but also
the hotel where I was staying, as well the taxi company
that had transported me here. He had been alerted to the
arrival of a man from his homeland.

His was also another rags-to-riches story, only on
a grander scale. The poorest relative in a large Sindhi
bhaiband family, he wanted to go as far away as possible to
escape the stigma of being poor. After knocking around for

a dozen years, trying this and that in Bombay, he arrived in Manaus one day with $5 in his pocket. And now, as I discovered the following day in the huge department store that he owned, he was the largest employer in Manaus, hugely respected and much loved by the locals. On the outside, he was no different from local residents, speaking Brazilian Portuguese without a trace of an accent. Inside, he was all Sindhi. His wife too was a purebred Sindhi, who served us a Sindhi lunch, and invited me afterwards to watch the latest Bollywood hit in their private movie theatre at home.

They had met at a typical Sindhi wedding in Bombay. By then, he had made good and was regarded as something of a 'catch' by Sindhi mothers of unwed daughters. The prestige that comes with business success is ranked the highest among the Sindhis, Falzon reminds us. The two married, and slowly over the years, he brought over countless cousins, nephews from his wife's and his own family. Many of them started out as his employees, learned the business and went on their own, often to compete with him.

My gracious host at lunch is typical of a Sindhi Hindu saga—enterprise, hard work and financial success. He was following 150-year-old tradition of mobility. Falzon describes how Sindhi adventurers in search of fortune set sail, embarking on voyages to new, unknown destinations to break into new places. They faced challenges, bravely and with equanimity, and create eventually a diasporic community of networks of family and fellow Sindhis. The story began in the eighteenth century among trading families, mainly in Shikarpur, who began posting young Sindhi boys in distant trading posts in places as far away as Porbandar, Aden, Kabul, Kandahar and Bukhara.

In the second half of the nineteenth century, *bhaiband* traders of Sindh Hyderabad discovered foreign demand for their local crafts and luxuries, just as the world was integrating into a global market as a result of British colonial rule and technological change created by the steamship and the telegraph. This is the fabled tale of Sindhwork that Falzon has described with panache in Chapter 3. By 1891, the diaspora of Sindhworks had spread to thirty-seven countries. By the time of Partition in mid-twentieth century, the Sindhwork global trade diaspora had become a thriving network of professionally managed firms such as the Chanrais, Chellarams and Choitrams. They offered opportunity to young Sindhis displaced by the Partition. Once there, many employees typically setup their own companies. As a result, opportunities had also multiplied because the diaspora had diversified into fields as distant and exotic as financing soap operas on television in Indonesia.

My host in Manaus no longer lives in South America. He has retired to a quiet, anonymous, upper-class life in a village in Surrey in the south of England, where he predictably cultivates his garden. His wife would have been happier returning to Mumbai, but he made friends with several Englishmen in his later years, and the Anglophile in him won out. He had impressed me as a deeply sensitive man, conscious of the loss that Sindhis had suffered in the Partition when they severed ties with the land of the Indus River. It was not so much the material loss, which they soon made good and surpassed exponentially. It was the irretrievable loss of a remembered homeland—its traditions, culture, and identity.

He spoke openly that afternoon about how Sindhis approached religion in a typically Hindu syncretic way. He showed me their 'puja room' where he and his wife meditated. I observed there a liberal mixture of Hinduism, Sikhism and Islam. The room proudly displayed photographs of the Radhasoami guru of the mystical sect of Beas in Punjab. Surprisingly, he also happened to be my father's guru, and we found suddenly that we were guru-bhais. There were photos of Nanak as well, and a copy of the Guru Granth Sahib—his father had been a Nanakpanthi in pre-partition Sindh. His wife had added plenty of images of Hindu gods.

In a moment of introspection, he spoke about the Sindhi stereotype—how his community was viewed as shallow, committed only to money and loving the flashy life. 'We don't offer an attractive face to the world, I realize. There is much truth in Sindhi bashing". But like any community, the stereotype hides more than it reveals. The average Sindhi, he said, was an ordinary human being, no different from others with his sorrows and joys.

The Story of Indian Business

This story of the Sindhis is the thirteenth volume in Penguin's multi-volume series, *The Story of Indian Business*. The series attempts to mine the great ideas of business and economics that have shaped commerce in the Indian bazaar and on the Indian Ocean over the centuries. Leading contemporary scholars have examined historical texts, inscriptions and records, and interpreted them in a lively manner for the thoughtful, intelligent reader. Each slender volume offers an enduring perspective on business enterprise to promote a longer-term sensibility regarding the material bases of our present human condition, what ancient Indians called *artha*.

The series began with Tom Trautmann's re-interpretation for our time of the renowned treatise on the science of wealth, *Arthashastra*, which was authored almost 2000 years ago and is considered the world's first manual in political economy. Kanakalatha Mukund took us south in the next volume, *The World of the Tamil Merchant*, to a beguiling trading world when a ship from Rome used to touch a south Indian port daily. Mukund has reconstructed this world by drawing on the epics, *Silappadikaram* and *Manimekalai* and other historical materials till the end of the Chola Empire. Next, we jumped a few centuries to Tirthankar Roy's account of the East India Company, which taught us, among other things, how much the modern multinational corporation is a child of a company that became a ruler in India and is mostly reviled today.

Our fourth volume hopped on to the late eighteenth century during the decline of the port of Surat and the rise of Bombay. In it, Lakshmi Subramanian recounted vividly the ups and downs in the adventurous lives of *Three Merchants of Bombay: Trawadi Arjunji Nathji, Jamsetjee Jeejeebhoy and Premchand Roychand*. Arshia Sattar returned to India's classical past to narrate in the fifth volume the charming adventures of *The Mouse Merchant* and other tales based on the eleventh century text, *Kathasaritsagara*, plus the *Panchatanra* and other sources. In the subsequent volume, Tom Timberg's *Marwaris* examined the bold, risk-taking world of the India's most famous business community, and it has quickly become a best seller.

In the seventh volume, Scott Levi took us back to the early modern period, recounting the saga of Punjabi Khatri traders from Multan, who took caravans on the 'silk road' across the Himalayas to Central Asia and beyond to Russia from 1500 to 1850. After that, Chayya Goswami and Jaitirath Rao dove deep with into the Indian Ocean in the eighteenth century to recount the tale of Gujarati merchants from Kachchh in the triangle trade between Mandvi, Muscat and Zanzibar. In the ninth volume, Omkar Goswami described a new way of organizing business—the managing agency—which was born in India with the decline of the East India Company and became popular both by the English and Indians for a century and a half.

The tenth volume by Bibek Debroy recounted how the railways were built and brought modernity to India, contributed to the of making a nation. *The Dharma of Business: Commercial Law in Medieval India* by the Sanskrit scholar, Donald Davis, was the eleventh volume. It dealt with the tension between morality and law, based on the Dharmashastras and commentaries on them. Finally, Medha Kudaisiya wrote the twelfth volume, recording a bitter-sweet tale of betrayal in the historic *Bombay Plan*, drawn by eminent industrialists in 1944–45 on the future shape of independent India's economy.

After the Sindhis will follow volumes on other trading communities: on the Chettiars by Raman Mahadevan, and on the Parsees by Rasheed Wadia. Prof Shalva Weill is writing on the Sassoon family in India. Future volumes will bring, among other riches, compelling tales of trade from Mughal India by Farhat Hasan and from the Indian Ocean by Sunil Amrith.

Gurcharan Das

1. WHO ARE THE SINDHIS?

'If you meet a Sindhi and a snake, kill the Sindhi first', goes the saying. It is as popular as it is derogatory, heaving with stereotype and not terribly original— the snake just as often finds itself ceding priority in such a choice to Jews and Marwaris in India, among other communities across the world. In many cases, what lends these groups their supposed venom is their reputation as hard-nosed entrepreneurs who will stop at nothing to make a buck. Certainly, this book rejects this 'wisdom'. It also rejects vague and unfounded generalizations that tar certain groups, in this case Sindhis, as undifferentiated masses of single-minded entrepreneurs. What it does argue is that the convergent histories of Sindhis earn them a peach of a place in the story of Indian business.

It is not the case that all Sindhis are in business. In the course of my work, I met Sindhi doctors, teachers, scientists, civil servants, artists, salaried employees of private companies and state institutions and so on. This, however, is a book about Sindhi business. It discusses the idea, well-trodden in both the popular imagination and in scholarly literature, that Sindhis are a 'business community': that is, that they constitute an ethnic group which is synonymous with business, and that they routinely tap into the resources of family and ethnicity (thus, 'community') in their pursuit of enterprise. The second characteristic that any work on Sindhis and Sindhi business must reckon with is mobility. While Sindhis are from India, they do not necessarily live in the country. Indeed, perhaps the most impressive thing about Sindhis is their geographical spread. They like to joke that when Neil Armstrong took his small step, he was approached by a Sindhi who tried to sell him a flag. More prosaically, scholars in the field invariably find themselves using words like 'global', 'transnational', 'diaspora' and 'cosmopolitan' in the context of Sindhis. This, then, is a story of Indian business, which, if not quite to the moon, will take us far beyond India.

But first, a word about the protagonists. In its broadest sense, the word 'Sindhi' refers to people who actually live in the region of Sindh, or who identify it as their homeland in ancestral-historical ways. Many speak the Sindhi language as a native tongue, or have ancestors who did so. The people of this book are, however, a more restricted sort. 'Sindhi' here refers to Hindu Sindhis with a family history of Partition exodus from Pakistan, and to their direct ancestors in pre-Partition Sindh. As of 2017, the province of Sindh in Pakistan had a population of around 48 million, of which, around 3.5 million (6.5 per cent) were Hindu and over 43 million (91.3 per cent) are Muslim; over three quarters of the Hindus lived in the rural areas of the province.[1] By and large—and there are voices to the contrary—the Sindhis of India and those in the diaspora elsewhere do not identify with this minority. And they certainly do not identify with the Muslim majority in Sindh. This is because the collective experience of Partition is so central to who they are that it singles them out as a group. To them, Sindh is a remembered homeland, and remembered intrinsically through the episode of Partition.

The homeland itself likely got its name from the river Indus, which for millennia has nourished agriculture and civilization. From 712 CE, the region was ruled by a succession of Muslim lords and dynasties. By the mid-nineteenth century, most of Sindh was under the control of the four dynastic branches of the Talpur Mirs, who had ousted the Kalhoras following the Battle of Halani in 1783. It was inevitable that the region would sooner or later catch the roving eye of the British, and in spring 1843, two bloody battles were fought at Miani (February) and Dubbo (March). The Mirs were defeated and deposed, and Sindh was annexed to the British possessions in the subcontinent that same year. At the time of annexation, about 75 per cent of the population was Muslim and the rest, mostly Hindu, though the equation was more balanced in the towns—in 1901, roughly four out of ten inhabitants in the main towns of Karachi, Hyderabad and Shikarpur in Sindh were Hindu.[2] This resonates with the fact that there was a considerable division of labour, with trade being predominantly in the hands of the Hindus. 'Trade' here includes activities as diverse as rural moneylending, small shopkeeping, and networks of highly mobile bankers and merchants who were based in the towns of Sindh but did business as far afield as in Central Asia, south India and, in the case of the celebrated 'Sindhworkis', many other places around the world.

While the Hindus of Sindh were never synonymous with the hierarchies and trappings of caste that structured society in other parts of India, there were certain significant distinctions. One was regionality. There were social differences, and sometimes hierarchies between the Sindhis from 'upper' (north) and 'lower' (south) Sindh, between those from the towns and the villages, and among the community in the towns. In some cases, these distinctions were based on narratives of historical origin. Thus, for example, the *amils* (see below) included an elite sub-group known as the 'Khudabadi amils', who supposedly could trace back their family roots to Khudabad, which in the eighteenth century served as the capital of the Kalhora dynasty. Another example is that of the Hindus of Hyderabad and Shikarpur, who certainly by the end of the nineteenth century saw themselves as different from other Sindhis in some ways. Partly this was because they specialized in distinct types of trade: the former in the transnational type known as Sindhwork, the latter in mobile banking and moneylending. The kind of trade a Sindhi did was, in fact, a second type of distinction and hierarchy. A third differentiation was based on different 'birth groups', which often mirrored further occupational specialization. Thus amils, who were associated mostly with Hyderabad and Karachi, were Hindus who leaned towards public service rather than trade. This role was historically rooted, since the Muslim Talpur Mirs had often employed highly literate Hindu amils in administration, revenue collection and other forms of public office. Under the British, the amils emerged as an Anglophiles, formally qualified (in law, and so on) as administrative elite. The Hindu bhaibands, on the other hand, were largely employed in trade, most notably in Sindhwork. In any case, these various distinctions were fluid as well as cross-cutting. Both these features exist even today—in the context of arranged marriages, for example, and in social and business connections.

As mentioned earlier, the story of Sindhi business is fundamentally one of mobility. If all mobilities are significant in one way or another, some are, as a contemporary anthropologist has put it, positively momentous.[3] Since well before 1947, Sindhis had travelled westward and to south India, in the case of the Shikarpuri moneylenders, and to port cities all over the world, in the case of the Sindhworkis. That part of the plot will be taken up in the chapters that follow, but the one set of events that changed the lives of all Sindhis was Partition of India. It was largely following the bloody riots of January 1948 that the bulk of Hindus in Sindh left their homes there and moved to India, or to places where they already had a history of partial settlement and business interests. For various logistical and administrative reasons (for one, Sindh had been part of the Bombay Presidency from 1843 to 1936),

Bombay received a large chunk of the refugees, in the
city itself and especially in the camp of Kalyan outside
the city. While the twin loss of home and belongings hit
hard and wide, as did the trauma of forced migration in
violent circumstances, the better-connected Sindhis—
notably the qualified amils, and the Sindhworkis and
Shikarpuri moneylenders with established business
offices in India—found it easier to adapt to life in their
new home. Broadly, their social and economic history
in Sindh meant that the bulk of the refugees eventually
settled in towns and cities, and most Sindhis in India
today are an urban people with a strong occupational
tendency towards trade.

Momentous as it was, Partition was by no means
the last wave of mobility experienced by the Sindhis.
Especially in the three decades after the Second World
War, substantial numbers (primarily from India) settled
in the United States, Britain, Canada and Australia.
In the last quarter of the twentieth century, the
commercial opportunities in the Gulf countries, notably
Dubai, attracted thousands of Sindhis. Less benign
were the 'numerous small partitions', as some Sindhis
call them, that have led to waves of mobility over the
years. Perhaps the most noteworthy was their movement
en masse out of east Africa from the late 1960s, when
political changes linked to programmes of so-called
'Africanization' effectively forced the thousands of Sindhi
traders who had been settled there since Partition, and in
many cases, before that, to relocate.

The upshot of these multiple mobilities is that one would be hard-pressed to find a country where there are no Sindhis at all. While they remember Sindh as the ancestral homeland, they relate to India, and especially to Mumbai, as a site of cultural renewal and interaction. Indeed, since Partition, Mumbai has emerged as a sort of cultural heartland for many Sindhis, especially among those who live outside of India; Mumbai is, as a Sindhi who lives in the city told me, 'a sea into which many rivers flow'. The city, with its commercial buzz and fun-loving soul, and of course, its sizeable and palpable Sindhi presence, is the kind of India they identify with. At the very least, they might visit every few years for a family wedding. These visits sometimes double as scouting trips which, with luck, produce good nuptial matches and further weddings. They also create the kind of informal settings where knowledge of how and where in the world to do business is circulated. Finally, Mumbai is a favoured venue for conspicuous consumption and philanthropy. In the case of the wealthier Sindhis, particularly the 'old money' Sindhworki families that control large transnational businesses, they may hold lavish weddings, and their largesse may include financial patronage of private hospitals, temples and religious gurus.

Lastly, 'Hindu' is not a word to be used shallowly for the Sindhis. In Sindh, in pre-Partition times, many Hindus were Nanakpanths. While not Khalsa Sikhs, they were devoted to the teachings of Guru Nanak, even as they worshipped the deities more usually associated with, for want of a better term, mainstream Hinduism. Not surprisingly, given the history of the region, many Hindu Sindhis were also followers of Sufi pirs. Typically, a Sindhi temple would include the Guru Granth Sahib of the Sikhs as well as images from the Hindu pantheon, without any particular discrimination between Shaivite and Vaishnavite deities. This is still the case with Sindhi temples around the world today, with two telling qualifiers. The first is that, increasingly, there is a tendency on the part of Sindhis to think of and represent themselves as Hindu through and through: the references to Sikhism and Sufism in their worship are not aspects they are generally keen to foreground, that is. The many reasons for this are beyond the scope of this book, but Rita Kothari, scholar and author, sums up one of them usefully: '... their Hinduness, the chief reason for their migration, was also put to question in states like Gujarat, Rajasthan and parts of Uttar Pradesh. As a community that ate meat and eschewed traditional Hindu practices such as untouchability, and hailed from "Pakistan", the Sindhis were considered "Muslim-like" and "untouchable" in staunch vegetarian states such as Gujarat and Rajasthan ... despite being a religious Hindu minority in Sindh, the Sindhis enjoyed far greater prestige and acceptance there than they did by becoming a Hindu community in a nation (implicitly, and in the division of subcontinent discourse) meant for Hindus'.[4]

Second, the post-Partition decades have seen the rise of Jhulelal as the *ishta devata* (preferred deity) of Hindu Sindhis worldwide. The devotion to Jhulelal—originally also known as Uderolal, among other appellations—has roots in pre-Partition Sindh, where he was revered as an avatar of the Hindu deity Varuna, who had saved local Hindus from the excesses of a tyrannical Muslim ruler. The evidence suggests that this devotion and the various rituals and observances were not widespread in Sindh: notably, they seem to have been largely unknown to the bhaibands and amils of Hyderabad and Karachi. Following Partition, and as part of an attempt to bring some coherence to the dispersed Sindhis and render them identifiable as a distinctive group in India and elsewhere, a group of cultural entrepreneurs revitalized Jhulelal and recast him as the God of all Hindu Sindhis. The project met with considerable success, and today the image of Jhulelal (typically, a bearded old man sitting on a lotus flower that in turn rests on a palla fish swimming in the Indus) is found in most Sindhi temples, homes and offices. Especially in India, including Mumbai, there are also Sindhi-run-and-attended temples where the main focus of devotion is Jhulelal. The attributed day of his birth on Cheti Chand marks, and is celebrated as the start of the New Year for Hindu Sindhis. Especially in India, but also in places where Sindhis are settled in significant numbers, feasts and events are often held to mark the occasion. Likewise, the Jhulelal-associated ritual known as 'bahrano sahib', which involves processions and water offerings (Varuna is classically associated with the sea), has travelled well. Together with the group-specific devotions to Sadhu T.L. Vaswani and Dada J.P. Vaswani, both Sindhi saints, the worship of Jhulelal has become a definitional element of Sindhi religious life.

Back to the story of Sindhi business: in spite of the popular fiction, there is no such thing as a Sindhi miracle. It is tempting in a book like this to levitate into hagiography and drop names like that of Parmanand Deepchand Hinduja, who in 1914, left Shikarpur for Bombay as a trader and moneylender, and who by 1919 had already set up a thriving branch of his business in Iran. His sons—Srichand, Gopichand, Ashok and Prakash—own and control a vast business empire that employs tens of thousands in a multitude of countries around the world. It would appear that what the Hindujas do not own, they do not want: their notable acquisitions include Gulf Oil in 1984, the automobile company Ashok Leyland in 1987, hotels, Swiss banks, hospitals, IT companies and much else. In 2014, they made it to the summit of the *Sunday Times* Rich List. In 2021, their estimated fortune of £17 billion meant they had to make do with a more modest third place on the List.

Feet back on the ground, the truth is rather a mixed bag. Some Sindhi businesses do very well indeed, and become sources of great wealth and prestige. Others do well enough to provide the people who own or run them with a decent living. Still, others do not, and the biographies of Sindhi businesses are also chronicles of false starts, failed ventures, and of money and friends lost. Take Gul Chatlani (pseudonym), who lives in a comfortable semi-detached house in north London. He was born into a family of small-time traders in Quetta, today the capital of the province of Balochistan, in 1934. When he was still in the cradle, an earthquake devastated the city and the family moved to Shikarpur and then on to Karachi. At Partition, the family left Sindh and spent a few years moving from place to place in south India before eventually settling in Bombay. Gul's first job was as an employee of Indian Railways, but 'something inside' told him it would not do. At the time, enterprising Sindhis were putting up blocks of apartments in the city on so-called 'ownership basis'. Sociable, and known in Sindhi circles as a trustworthy man, Gul saw his chance. It was a rocky start, but things got better, and by the 1960s he had cobbled together enough capital to try his hand at film financing, which at the time was another Sindhi speciality. It proved a disastrous decision, one that left him all but penniless. One day, however, through his brother-in-law who happened to be visiting Bombay, he met a Lebanese man who ran businesses in Sierra Leone, where Gul's sister's marital family lived. One thing led to another, and before long, Gul was on a plane to Africa to run a regional car dealership for his new-found friend. It was a productive move, except that in 1974, the oil crisis struck and he could not sell a single car. He moved back to India with his family, and then to London to, as he put it, 'start a new chapter'. There he ran a shop and eventually a small supermarket. He also dabbled in and invested in real estate, not entirely without success. That was until the property crash of the late 1980s hit him hard and he again lost a lot of money. His pension, and whatever savings he had left, made it possible for him to retire soon after.

Mixed bags make for hierarchies, and certainly the prestige that comes with business success is ranked among Sindhis. I was once talking to a man who had just retired from a salaried job with a telephone company, when a well-known Sindhi religious leader walked past without greeting him. 'Look at him,' came the bitter comment, 'He would certainly have stopped to talk to me if I had been rich.' Or take Laju Choitram (pseudonym), a modestly successful businessman, who was discussing with his wife that maybe they should cut expenses on their daughter's wedding by holding the reception at a mandir rather than a five-star hotel. 'Consider the trouble this will create,' he told her, 'People will come and say "I am Ramchand, I am a big businessman, I only drink Black Label, and I do not want to sit there with those people"'. The Sindhis universally looked up to are almost always wealthy and from well-established business families. The high prestige that business is held in comes across in marriage-matching, too. Many matrimonial advertisements in the *Times of India* and internet websites carry the words 'well settled in business'. There are other occupations that are considered desirable—some of the professions (especially medicine and engineering) and information technology stand out—but by and large, the person who does well in business is most eligible. As one woman told me, 'A good match is what matters. If one is educated, the match should be educated—like that. Naturally, business is particularly well regarded.' Coming up in the business world is seen as the ultimate marker of personal ability and worth: 'What would

I look for in a match for my daughter? I'll tell you: will and the strength to succeed. My daughter is married to a Sindhi based in Nigeria, and her husband owns four plastics factories. He was originally evicted together with his family from Cambodia, and they fled to India and eventually to Nigeria where he established a business. He started out in poverty and eventually succeeded.'

While it is hard to speak of a typical Sindhi business life, this book does suggest that there are some family resemblances. The first is the compulsion to strike out on one's own. While Sindhis do often take up jobs in the private or public sector, many describe an urge, as much individual as socially sanctioned, to set up in self-employed business. This is how Lal, who runs his own small company in Mumbai, put it: 'Every community has something in its genes. I once worked in accounts in a private company. I enjoyed the work, but I was also miserable. My grandfather used to tell me that I was not cut out to work for people and that I should start my own business. You grow up listening to conversations about business, this and that business, every evening at dinner, and your mind takes you in that direction. Today, if someone offered me a job on double my income, I would turn it down. I would not be doing my own thing.' Clearly, this tendency is a double-edged sword. While employment of kin and co-ethnics has historically been one of the key means by which Sindhi businesses could grow, it also presents the risk that employees will strike out on their own, often to compete in the same lines. One of my sources in London, Sham (pseudonym), saw exactly this happen in the electronics trade in Panama, and he himself had left the family clothing business in 1996 to set up his own business in a similar line; as he put it, 'You employ a Sindhi, you pay the price.'

A second community trait is the readiness to take risks, coupled with a certain ability to bounce back when things go wrong. Again, Lal had something to say about this: 'My grandfather taught me that even if you lose everything, maintain your reputation and composure and shrewdness and you will come back; in business you will make losses, but you will also make gains.' The twin themes of perseverance and resilience are rehearsed in a neat metaphor by Sindhi author Nandu Asrani. He should know, because, in his own candid words, 'I have tried many business ventures, investments, and entered all kinds of fields, including sports. I succeeded in some—and failed in many.' Discarding the snake chestnut, Asrani proposes an alternative—and infinitely more productive—zoology as a metaphor for his people:

> The correct analogy for a Sindhi is a spider . . . A spider painstakingly weaves a web, and if it breaks or is destroyed, it falls. But silently, without fuss, it gets up and starts all over again. And a spider does this innumerable times, right through its life. This is the true spirit of a Sindhi, who gets up, starts afresh, maybe this time finding a different spot or place to make the web, not afraid to rebuild again![5]

Perhaps the metaphor is doubly pertinent, as one of the reasons why Sindhis have a knack for surviving hard knocks is that they build symbiotic webs. This is, in fact, the third community trait: at any point in their business lives, and especially when things get difficult, Sindhis often find that they can draw on their networks of family, friends and co-ethnics to regain access to all-important resources like credit. To describe Sindhis as a kind of hippy commune would be to caricature them. At the same time, the story of Sindhi business strongly suggests that there is in fact, a current of mutual benefit that individual businesses can and do tap into, usually episodically. Finally, no understanding of Sindhi business would be complete without an emphasis on the fact that, historically as well as today, mobility is of the essence.

These, then, are the community traits that underwrite the story I shall be telling in the chapters that follow. The guiding question asked in this book is not why Sindhi businesses always succeed. They do not. Rather, the question is: how have histories come together to make a people who, for hundreds of years and in a variety of ways, have been synonymous with business and entrepreneurship, wherever they are found?

2. BEGINNINGS

One morning in 1805, a group of Sindhi merchants, together with their wives and children and an entourage of 'up to two thousand', left their homes in Karachi on a pilgrimage to Hinglaj, about 250 km to the north. They stayed there for two-and-a-half months, during which time they spent 'large sums of money in charity and in feeding Brahmins and fakirs' and 'acquired such renown on account of their liberality that Bhats and Brahmans chanted their benevolence in songs especially composed'. They were the family of Seth Naomul Hotchand (1804–78), who would go on to achieve considerable notoriety in certain circles as a collaborator of the British in Sindh. Fortunately for us, he also wrote his memoirs.[1]

Whatever his political sympathies, Naomul was not one to undersell his silver spoon. He makes it known that by the time he was born, his family already owned agencies and firms 'at about 500 places', mainly in north India and around the Arabian Sea. Originally from the district of Dadu in Sindh, the family had been renowned for its wealth and business prowess at least since the late seventeenth century, when Naomul's great-great-grandfather, Sujanmal, owned 'a large estate in zamindari . . . (and) was besides a great merchant and banker, enjoyed a good name, and great respect among the townspeople'. His son, Nanukdas, 'placed his gumashtas at Shah Bandar, Tatta, Sonmiani, Beyla, Shikarpur, and Chandka'. A family dispute caused Nanukdas's son, Bhojoomal, to leave his father's home and business—but not relinquish his father's business model—and to settle in the small port of Kharakbunder, a small port near what is today, Karachi. He soon set up gumashtas (agents) at Sonmiani, Gwadur, Beyla and Muscat; in turn, his gumashta at Muscat opened branches at Bushire, Shiraz and Bahrain. Through the ports of Shahbunder and Lahoribunder, business was conducted with Surat, Porebunder and Malabar. In 1749, Bhojoomal's sons, who by now were running the show jointly with their uncle Kewalram following their father's death, placed a gumashta in Bombay, and through him traded with Bengal and China. Their agent at Muscat traded with Persia, Bassorah and Bahrain, and they had other agencies at Kabul, Kandahar, Herat, Khelat and Kashmir. Naomul reassures us that 'the members of this family acted in perfect concord, which secured them great honour and influence, and their whole conduct of affairs partook of the appearance of a petty government. They possessed a common storehouse for provisions of all kinds, tents of sorts, and furniture of variety . . . The annual private expenditure of the household at Karachi amounted to Rs 40,000 inclusive of what was paid to the gumashtas'.

Naomul's account of the glory, wealth and amity of his forebears is perhaps not to be taken too literally. The point is, however, that it affords us a rare glimpse into the aspirations—if not necessarily their actual outcomes—of traders in eighteenth- and nineteenth-century Sindh. It suggests that the model of building a family business by posting agents at strategic trading points was well established among the Hindu Sindhi traders, and had been for some time. It was the system that would later underwrite the Sindhwork trade diaspora, for one. Equally telling are Naomul's descriptions of a business family hiving off sons to distant places, as well as of the routes by which wealth was put to conspicuous use through patronage and largesse back home.

The pitfall of going by longue durée narratives is the tendency to not mind the gaps. To suggest that there is an unbroken and direct line between Naomul, his distant ancestors, and say, a Sindhi hotelier in Kuala Lumpur in 2021, would be to indulge in creative genealogy. The point is rather to locate Naomul and the hotelier within a regional tradition of mobility and trade that stretches back centuries, albeit in a chequered way. Certainly, in the case of Sindh, the sources all point in that direction: by Naomul's time, the region's ports had periodically functioned as nodes in the Indian Ocean and Arabian Sea trade networks for quite some time. Possibly the earliest source of information on this is the geographer Al-Idrisi (1100–1165/66), who produced accounts of Sindh, its cities and their trade. For example, he describes the town

of Daybul (Debal): '. . . the commercial activities of
. . . (whose) people are of a varied nature and they
deal in diverse commodities'; the port functioned
as an entrepôt, where Omani as well as Chinese
and Indian traders brought in Chinese cloth, Indian
aromatics, perfumes and other goods, which local
merchants bought wholesale and later resold, often in
distant places. Al-Mansurah, which was located close
to present-day Hyderabad in Pakistan, is described
as 'a big town with a large population and wealthy
merchants'. Al-Ror and Sharusan (situated in present-
day Rohri and Sehwan, respectively) were both large
towns with thriving populations of merchants and
busy markets that were much frequented by visitors.[2]

Centuries later, the Sindhi Sufi mystic and poet
Shah Abdul Latif (1689–1752) wrote of the merchants
of his homeland and of their journeys in pursuit
of trade. They apparently usually set off after the
monsoon, with the onset of favourable winds: their
boats oiled and made ready, they celebrated Diwali at
home in Sindh and left immediately after, often for
months at a time. Their journeys took them to places
as far apart as Porbandar in Gujarat and Aden in Yemen.
In Sri Lanka, they traded in precious materials, and they
sometimes went further afield, to the Far East. Latif's
lyrical descriptions are anything but dry: we learn
of the lamentations of women left behind in Sindh,
of pirates and heavy seas, and of goods spoiled on
journeys that proved too ambitious.[3]

There are more prosaic sources, too. The records
of the Dutch East India Company (Vereenigde

Oostindische Compagnie, VOC) from the seventeenth and eighteenth centuries abound with references to Sindhi traders and their practices, including that of acting as brokers for the European trading companies. One incident described here happened in 1757, when the Dutch merchant Brahe met a group of Hindu traders from 'Karaatje' (Karachi) through a local broker called 'Annendramme' (Anand Ram). Upon careful inspection of Brahe's stock of spices and sugar, they offered to buy it—on one condition. They could easily get the same goods at better prices from the English, they informed Brahe, and would only buy from him if he gave them two-to-three months' credit. Probably in no position to negotiate, Brahe found some consolation in describing the traders, now his satisfied debtors, as a 'very parsimonious, suspicious and wary people'.[4]

These are fragmentary sources, to be sure, but I think they serve to give us some idea of the legacy of mobile trade that Sindhis can lay considerable claim to. I should properly say 'some groups of Sindhis'. It would not do to generalize, but it does make sense to build some historical understanding of the demography of trade and mobility in Sindh. By the last years of the rule of the Talpur Mirs, in the mid-nineteenth century, Hindus made up roughly a fourth of the total population of Sindh. However, because of the particular division of labour that existed, the significance of the group was out of proportion to its size. Occupationally, the population of Sindh under the Talpurs was made up of three types. The first type consisted of the landed elites, the Mirs themselves, who held large tracts of agricultural land and wooded areas set aside specially for hunting; the *waderos* or large landowners drawn from a hereditary Muslim aristocracy; and a sizeable number of smallholders. By Indian standards, the tracts of land held by the waderos were large. In order to qualify as a wadero, one had to own at least 500 acres, and many had holdings of 10,000 acres to 20,000 acres. The power wielded by the waderos in their rural estates could be immense, and depended on their individual wealth and prestige as well as their ability to enrol the allegiance of the second occupational type—the *haris* (agricultural workers and labourers) and the craftsmen—and of the owners of the small landholdings around the great estates.[5]

In the case of the waderos, the land was held by Muslims. Smaller holdings were less exclusively in Muslim hands. It appears that significant numbers of Hindus, and especially moneylenders, did indeed own land, not least through the forfeiture of mortgages. Contemporary accounts mention that some Hindus owned land in zamindari,[6] and that their numbers grew during the British period. One must keep in mind, however, that the prestige attached to land ownership meant that wealthy and socially aspirational Hindu traders were keen to weave it into their family histories. Naomul's account of his great-great-grandfather, Sujanmal, comes to mind.

The third occupational type was where the people of this book hail from. It is that of shopkeepers, merchants, traders and moneylenders—the businesspeople, or banias. In Sindh, at least until Partition, business and commerce were overwhelmingly the preserve of Hindus. One kind of business they ran was moneylending, both rural and trade-related. In Sindh, as in other parts of India, an elaborate edifice of credit brought together landowners, farmers and moneylenders, in ways that were not always risk-free or profitable to the lenders. However great their prestige, the waderos routinely depended on credit advanced by the banias in order to sustain their lifestyles and assert their status. The smaller zamindars, and indeed farmers themselves, were equally embedded in credit relationships with the rural moneylenders. When things went well, the banias secured a reliable and enduring supply of rural produce, which often made it possible for them to combine moneylending and trade. When they went badly, the banias could find themselves owning land through the forfeiture of mortgages. It was one means by which traders came to double as zamindars, especially with the Mirs out of the way from the mid-nineteenth century.[7] Throughout Sindh, then, the farming done by the cultivators (Muslims, for the large part) was economically and socially inseparable from the 'farming' carried out by (Hindu, mostly) moneylenders, who cultivated long-term relationships of credit and thus secured well-rooted incomes.

With respect to trade, the main hubs in Sindh before its annexation by the British were the port town of Karachi in the south, which had replaced Thatta as the main commercial centre in the later decades of the eighteenth century, and the town of Shikarpur in the north. Karachi had only begun to find its calling

as a port around the mid-eighteenth century. Seth
Naomul recounts how in 1729, a group of Hindu
banias—led by his ancestors, predictably—had been
the first to settle from other parts of Sindh there
in significant numbers, mainly on account of the
silting up of Kharakbunder. A nineteenth-century
source tells us that around 1813, the population of
Karachi had increased by more than half in less than
five years.[8] By 1843, Thomas Postans, army officer
and later administrator, was able to call Karachi the
'principal port' of Sindh and to describe the richness
of its cargoes. Its merchants, who in many cases were
also moneylenders, had trade itineraries that included
Bombay, Muscat, Surat, Kutch, Malabar and Basra. The
large variety of goods imported into Sindh included
metals (iron, tin, steel, lead and copper), foodstuffs
(tea, sugar, spices, coconuts and areca nuts) and
textiles (chintz, muslin, gold cloth and broad cloth),
as well as items like glass and china. From the west—
Persia, Khorassan, Arabia—came luxuries such as fine
weapons, carpets, dates, coffee, conserves and rose
water. Equally abundant was the list of products of local
or regional origin exported from Karachi: saltpetre,
salt, rice, cotton, ghee, oil, shark fins, calico and felts.
There were also goods imported from the north for
re-export elsewhere: asafoetida, saffron, horses, leather,
musk, alum, Kashmir shawls, dried fruit and precious
stones.[9] The quays at Karachi must have presented
a real assault on the senses. It is this world that the

wealthy and mobile merchants of Karachi, some of whom owned vessels, inhabited.

The commercial verve of the port of Karachi had a counterpart in Shikarpur, about 400 km to the north. Rather than for the exuberance of its maritime cargoes, the town was renowned for its merchant-moneylenders, whose story has been pieced together in the exemplary work of the French historian, Claude Markovits.[10] British travellers' accounts of the early-to-mid-nineteenth century describe the town, and its bazaars and mobile traders, in vivid detail. In the words of James McMurdo (one of the British travellers), for example, 'they are principally bankers, and possess a good deal of influence both with government and with the people. These Multanis carry on a trade with Kabul, Kandahar, Kuelat, Multan, and Bahamalpur'.[11] In 1837, Alexander Burnes, explorer and diplomat, wrote: '. . . it will only be necessary to name the towns at which the Shikarpoor merchants have agents to judge of the unlimited influence which they can command.'[12] That the bankers of Shikarpur were sometimes referred to as 'Multanis', especially in earlier sources, suggests that at least some had originally migrated from Multan (today an administrative division of the province of Punjab in Pakistan). It appears, however, that the rise of Shikarpur attracted traders from a number of places besides Multan. In fact, Markovits describes Shikarpur in the second half of the eighteenth century as a kind of 'bania melting pot', where merchants and bankers of different origins settled, and over time, developed a distinct Shikarpuri identity. The rise of Shikarpur as a centre of bania activity was one aspect of the town's transformation into the financial capital of the Durrani empire. Kandahar, the first Durrani capital, was well linked with Shikarpur through the Bolan Pass, a staple route of the camel caravans moving between north India and Central Asia. By the early nineteenth century, Shikarpur was the centre of an extended network of merchants and bankers encompassing most of Central Asia, and Shikarpuri hundis were known, recognized and circulated very widely indeed. The main business of the Shikarpuri bankers was to act as middlemen between the merchants of Bukhara and those of north India: silk moved in the direction of India, and indigo constituted the bulk of the return trade.

It has been suggested that, following the collapse of the Durrani hegemony in 1809, the business of the Shikarpuris took a dent. On one occasion in 1836, a 'large body of well-dressed and respectable-looking Hindoos from Shikarpore' complained to the British Political Agent for the Affairs of Sindh—not without hyperbole, it would seem—that the 'once-flourishing trade between Sinde (Upper) and Khorassan was utterly ruined; that immense quantities of merchandize formerly passed through Shikarpore, which was just now almost deserted from the dread of the Sikhs . . . that the promises and assurances of Runjeet Sing, the Ameers of Sinde, the chiefs of Cabool [Kabul], Candahar [Kandahar], and Peshawar, and the Prince (Wallee) of Herat, were all of a piece, and equally false and faithless; that no trader could venture to depend on them;

that they always had an excuse ready for exactions'.[13] It is, of course, risky to reach hard conclusions on the basis of such disconnected sources. Markovits cautions that early nineteenth-century British accounts peddled something of a 'myth of Shikarpur', and there is no reason to suppose that the decline thesis was any more rooted in fact. Whatever the state of their Central Asian trade, at the time of the British annexation of Sindh, the banias of Shikarpur had extended their activities to other, often distant parts of the subcontinent and elsewhere through the port of Karachi.

There are other clues that suggest that the Central Asian trade had not, in fact, been as utterly ruined as the respectable delegation complained it was. At the time of the Russian conquest of central Asia in the second half of the nineteenth century, the number of Shikarpuris trading in the region and the geographical extent of their networks were actually increasing, irrespective of the regime change. The sources point to the khanate of Bukhara (in present-day Uzbekistan) as the main destination and site of settlement of the Shikarpuris, who were apparently widely dispersed here. There were Shikarpuri traders doing business as far away as in Sinkiang (today Xinjiang, in north-western China), Iran and Afghanistan, among other places, besides Bukhara. This was no mean feat of mobility. As Markovits notes, it was far easier in the nineteenth century to travel from India by sea (as the Sindhworkis did, for example) than to travel overland between Shikarpur and Central Asia.

The journey would have taken these intrepid men across mountains, deserts, and the bandit-ridden regions of Afghanistan and south-eastern Iran. While their activities varied, according to the circumstances of their location, at least some were involved in a kind of trade by which grain was procured through moneylending and sold, apparently at a better profit and lower risk than they could have back in Sindh. The merchant-moneylending enterprise included Shikarpuris who ran large-scale banking businesses in the towns, who acted as brokers, and some who worked as smaller moneylenders who used money borrowed from larger-scale fellow Shikarpuris to conduct a trade in rural moneylending. The different tiers functioned as a whole through the gumashta-shah system, the richest shahs usually based in Shikarpur and the smaller ones and gumashtas in foreign lands.

Of course, it was not all about long-distance mobile trade and banking. Many Hindu Sindhis did business at home, often making use of camel caravans or riverine transport on the Indus to ferry cargo within Sindh. Records of customs litigations from just before the British annexation of Sindh give us some idea of the kinds of goods traded in and around Sindh: wheat purchased in the Sudder Bazaar at Sukkur to be taken by boat and sold at Larkana, a boatload of ghee transported from Abadpur to Sukkur and so on.[14] This trade in agricultural produce, itself often procured through the exchanges involved in rural moneylending, probably accounted for much of the business of Hindu banias in rural Sindh. They were small traders, far removed from (and yet connected to) the urban merchants of Karachi and the large-scale bankers of Shikarpur. Which is not to say that rural banias were necessarily of modest means or lacked local influence: rather, the point is that they did not quite enjoy the prestige that came with mobility and long-distance commerce. This distinction still lingers among Sindhis today, and especially so among the more internationally connected Sindhworkis, who are wont to make the point that their ancestors back in Sindh were wealthy urban merchants—as opposed to 'village banias'. The truth value of this sort of genealogy is anybody's guess. What matters is the premium placed on narratives of mobile and adventurous trade.

Pre-Partition Sindh, then, was a region with a Muslim majority where commerce was largely the preserve of the Hindus. It was a point that was not lost on contemporary sources, which tend to be fairly ambivalent in their judgement. Characteristically, British commentaries were contemptuous of what they saw as the innate and insatiable avarice of the Hindu banias. This is how the scholar and explorer Richard Francis Burton put it in 1877:

The typical man is a small, lean, miserable-looking wretch, upon whose wrinkled brow and drawn features, piercing black eye, hook-nose, thin lips, stubbly chin and half-shaven cheeks of crumpled parchment, Avarice has so impressed her signet that every one who sees may read. His dress is a tight little turban, once, but not lately, white, and a waistcloth in a similar predicament; his left

shoulder bears the thread of the twice-born, and a coat
of white paint, the caste-mark, decorates his forehead;
behind his ear sticks a long reed pen, and his hand swings
a huge rosary—token of piety, forsooth! That man is
every inch a Hindu trader.[15]

Even so, a number of post-annexation British
sources give long lists of the cruelties that Hindus
were said to have been subjected to under the Mirs:
forced circumcision, heavy taxation, beatings and all
manner of humiliation. The available evidence tends
not to support these claims. Hindu amils, for one, had
held high positions as scribes and revenue collectors
in Talpur Sindh. As McMurdo wrote around 1813,
'Hindus possess the confidence of the rulers, equally,
and perhaps in a greater degree than do the followers
of Muhammad; and they compose the most valuable
and trustworthy part of their establishment, as officers
and servants.'[16] It is likely that British accounts of the
injustice suffered by Hindus at the hands of the Mirs
were in fact none-too-subtle propaganda, concocted
to help them digest the inconvenient truth that they
had overthrown the Muslim rulers of Sindh in two
bloody and unprovoked battles. (General Charles
Napier, the conqueror of Sindh, is said to have sent
a telegram back home that read simply 'Peccavi'—a
wordplay on 'I have sinned/Sindh'.) Whatever the
morality of the conquest, it was an event that would give
rise, directly or otherwise, to what is perhaps the most
remarkable part of our story: the rise of Sindhwork.

3. THE SINDHWORKIS OF HYDERABAD

The story of Sindhwork is that of Sindhis at their most trailblazing. In the mid-nineteenth century, the Hindu traders of Hyderabad discovered that there was a foreign demand for the work of the craftsmen of Sindh—literally, 'Sindh work'. I will keep, as the main protagonist of my story, the individual entrepreneur, on the lookout for opportunities at all times. In this case, a number of historical circumstances and events crossed paths to make opportunities more likely to come about. When they did, the Hindu Sindhi entrepreneurs were in the right place at the right time. That place was a region that, following the deposition of the Talpur Mirs and annexation, found itself increasingly integrated into a global market, enabled by technologies of mobility and communication.

All evidence points towards Hyderabad as the birthplace of Sindhwork. In the mid-nineteenth century, the town, unlike Shikarpur and Karachi, was not a major commercial centre. It had a thriving bazaar and had a merchant community, to be sure, but it was not well known for its long-distance trade or banking. The one thing it did stand out for was as the seat of the Talpur Mirs. Courts tend to have healthy appetites for luxury, and that gave the town a certain edge in the artisanal goods trade. Travellers' accounts of Sindh from the first half of the nineteenth century invariably remark on the splendour of the court of the Talpur Mirs. Even allowing for a certain degree of hyperbole ('oriental' princes will have splendid courts), it is clear that the Mirs liked to surround themselves with objects of luxury, beauty and impeccable craftsmanship. James Burnes, who visited the court in 1819, was awestruck by the Mirs' wealth, which included embroidered textiles, personal ornaments, enamelled firearms and other weapons used for hunting.[1] The booty seized by the British in 1843 contained items such as a bridle set in mother-of-pearl, gold and precious stones, a pair of slippers with 166 pearls and emeralds sewn into the fabric, 167 gold matchlocks, gold and jewelled bedposts, and hundreds of other such objects.[2]

This is hardly surprising, considering that Sindh, among other places in India, generally enjoyed a reputation for the quality of its artisanal wares. For one, the region had a long tradition of luxury textile production, and embroidered cloth was a staple in gift exchange, especially among the wealthier classes.[3] Writing in 1816, Pottinger mentions that the principal manufactures of Hyderabad were arms—matchlocks, spears and swords—and embroidered lungis. He was impressed by the quality of the workmanship and noted that the production of firearms alone provided employment for a fifth of the population of the suburbs.[4] The upshot is that the court of the Mirs was the prime mover behind Hyderabad's preeminence in the manufacture of and trade in crafts. Beside the products of Sindh itself, the Mirs were also fond of imported luxury goods. They regularly wore English cloth and European damask silk, for example,[5] which meant yet another opportunity for the town's traders.

The deposition of the Mirs by the British changed all of that: suddenly, demand was all but gone. A contemporary official source gives us an indication of how the change affected the Hindu traders who had been supplying the court and its satellites:

The amil class, embroiderers, goldsmiths, dealers in silk and velvets, the tradesmen of the court, are all much worse off . . . Traders have probably found the demand for articles of Eastern luxury, in which they traded, much lessened by the removal of the princes and their families . . . The higher classes of Mahomedan and of Hindoo merchants, together with the manufacturers of loongees, embroidered cloths, gold and silver ornaments, swords, and all who in any way depended upon the Ameers and their courtiers, have lost by the change of Government . . . Also, all importers, vendors and manufacturers of swords, guns, daggers, cloths, stuffs, articles of jewellery, gold and silver ornaments, & c.; all of whom must have enjoyed a considerable amount of patronage from the Meers and their court, from the constant demand for arms of all sorts, khilats, presents, ornaments for their women, and stage equipage of every description.[6]

The situation in Hyderabad at the annexation of Sindh by the British was troubling for the Hindu traders and moneylenders. For decades, they had sourced luxury goods and artisanal wares from all over Sindh and beyond, and purveyed them to the court of the Mirs. The wares, or at least the capacity to make or procure them, were still there. What did not exist any longer was the market that had lapped them up. As for the moneylenders, it was now no longer possible to advance loans to the Talpur state.

But the annexation was as much a beginning as it was an end. Hyderabad had lost its Mirs, but it had gained its British—and it was precisely that chance that seems to have caught the eye of the Hindu traders. Certainly they had reason to believe that the artisanal wares of Sindh would read well in the new chapter. As we have seen, British travellers had long valued them highly, to the extent that they would on occasion go so far as to commission pieces for private purchase. This, however, was only part of the story. What really mattered was that the annexation embedded Hyderabad, and Sindh more broadly, into a rapidly expanding world economy, dominated and integrated by British interests. More than it had ever been, Hyderabad was now part of a world market, itself kept alive by ever-increasing flows of people, goods and information.

Communications and transport were key to this shift. In 1856, for instance, work started on the Karachi harbour improvement, which included dredging and the building of a breakwater. On land, the Karachi-to-Kotri section of the Sindh railway was opened in 1861. Around the same time, the Oriental Inland Steam Company was tasked with setting up the Indus Steam Flotilla, which would establish steamboat connections on the Indus; this apparently met with little success, but it did pave the way for the Indus Valley Railways, which eventually linked up with the major lines in India to connect Karachi to Delhi. The circuit was completed in 1889, with the opening of a bridge across the Indus at Sukkur. In 1864, the Indo-European Telegraph Department laid a 1300-mile-long submarine cable between Karachi and Fao (in what was then Turkish Arabia), thus joining the Turkish line of telegraph and linking Sindh (Karachi) to Europe.[7] Perhaps the most consequential of the works was the completion of the Suez Canal in 1871, which brought about a great and rapid increase in the volume of maritime mercantile activity in Karachi. In 1891–92, for instance, foreign trade in Sindh included thirty-seven countries, as compared with eighteen in 1871–72.[8] Sindh generally, and Hyderabad specifically, were now better connected than they ever had been, not least through improved links with the commercial hub that was Bombay.

This, then, was a world that was rapidly becoming more integrated and densely networked, in part due to the 'policy of adventure' and cultivation of free trade championed—and, in many ways, enforced—by the

British. This period, which has been described as a second industrial revolution, was one in which a number of different technological, political and social processes converged to create new forms of production, mobility, trade and communication, and to boost old ones. There was freedom of movement too, especially within the British hegemony, for British Indian subjects, as Sindhis now were.

This point cannot be overemphasized, because it is essential to our understanding of the origins of Sindhwork. While the broadening of networks beyond Sindh (usually via Bombay) by the Hyderabadi traders may in some or other measure have been a function of local circumstances, it was only feasible thanks to the global shifts of the latter half of the nineteenth century. It is not enough to locate the Sindhwork diaspora at origin: rather, it only begins to make sense when their destinations, as well as the dynamics that bound the two together, are taken into account. Thus, for example, Sindhworkis would not have found a lucrative market in Singapore (then the Straits Settlements), had this once-insignificant port not become an entrepôt of world trade under British occupation. Likewise, the trade by Sindhworkis in Indian textiles was made possible by the improved connections between Sindh and Bombay, as well as by the growing production by the Bombay mills of textiles for export to Zanzibar, Mauritius, Aden, German East Africa, Persia, Hong Kong, Shanghai, Arabia and the Straits Settlements, among other places.[9] The point is not that trade and specialized production, and links with Bombay and elsewhere, had not existed before, but rather that the British commercial and political hegemony presented an ever-broadening space in which the Sindhis could flourish and expand their business. A Hyderabadi trader who wished to explore new markets had a wider choice of destinations from Karachi harbour; an agent of a Sindhwork firm could relay a telegraph from Alexandria to the head office in Hyderabad in a few hours; and a Sindhworki plying a trade in 'oriental curios' in the Mediterranean found that the ports along the Suez Canal route presented a necklace of opportunities.

From around 1860, we find Hyderabadi Sindhworki traders doing business far and wide. They first arrived in Japan a few years after the 1868 Meiji Restoration;[10] a Sindhwork firm was plying its trade in Malta at least as early as in the 1880s; a merchant called Bulchand from Hyderabad set ashore on the Gold Coast, in what today is Ghana,[11] in the 1890s; and Ceylon (Sri Lanka) got its first Sindhi traders in 1880.[12] Sindhis set up business in Gibraltar in 1870; in Sierra Leone via the Mediterranean in 1893;[13] and in Hong Kong, 'a small Sindhi community was active by the late 1920s . . . although some arrived earlier'.[14]

The first long-range target of the Sindhwork diaspora seems to have been the Mediterranean, via Bombay. Claude Markovits holds that the original destinations were Egypt, India and the Far East, in that order.[15] A descendant of Pohoomull Pohkhiani, the first of the old family firms in Gibraltar to open business there, agrees: 'Pohoomull and his brothers went into ports, that's where the steamships would go. Egypt was the first port of call, it was very important. The natural choice of expansion westward was Egypt: Cairo, Alexandria. And then from there on they ventured out, as far as to Panama. Today you find them everywhere.'[16] It is not difficult to see why the Mediterranean was so attractive. While not quite yet the kingdom of package holidays and crowded beaches it is today, the Mediterranean was by then already a favourite destination with travellers and tourists from Britain and the other industrialized countries of northern Europe, and therefore a potentially profitable market for wares that felt artisanal, authentic and exotic. Even before construction of the Suez Canal, the overland route from Europe through the Mediterranean and the Red Sea was popularized around 1840, most prominently by the Peninsular and Oriental Steam Navigation Company (later P&O). Passengers would embark at the ports of the north and sail through Gibraltar, disembarking at Alexandria and proceeding by Nile steamer to Cairo; from Cairo, they went by carriage to Suez, where they took another boat down the Red Sea and frequently a third at Aden, depending on whether their final destination was Bombay, Calcutta or Madras.[17] Tellingly, these names come up again and again in the papers of Sindhwork firms of the mid-to-late nineteenth century.

Apart from its obvious advantages, mobility was fundamental to the Sindhworkis also because as they moved, they discovered and developed new supply-demand combinations. In the late nineteenth century, their trade in curios and silk increasingly drew upon sources other than the local (and increasingly limited) production of Sindh. They tapped into supply points in India and the Far East, particularly Bombay—where many Sindhwork firms set up depots and, in some cases, offices—and Japan. The firms were quick to open new branches and expand their networks in places as far apart as Panama and Australia. Not surprisingly, their itineraries often overlapped with the routes of the British empire. Suffice it to look at the letterheads of a sample of ten firms operating around 1917. (This was a time of war, and some of the requests for freedom of movement eventually found their way into the national archives in Malta.) Their itineraries included Colón, Port of Spain and Valparaíso in south and central America; Malta, Gibraltar, Tangier, Ceuta, Melilla, Algiers, Tunis, Genoa, Naples, Palermo, Catania, Tripoli, Benghazi, Alexandria, Port Said, Cairo, Luxor and Aswan in and around the Mediterranean; Mombasa, Zanzibar, Delagoa Bay and Durban in Africa; Quetta, Karachi, Hyderabad-Sindh, Bombay, Calcutta and Madras in the Indian subcontinent; Kobe, Tsingtao, Shanghai, Hong Kong, Penang, Singapore, Sukabumi and Bandung in the rest of Asia; and Melbourne in Australia.

The case of the small Mediterranean island of Malta, which at the time was part of the British empire, is particularly well documented. The earliest known record of Sindhworkis in Malta dates from 1887, when the firm Pohoomull Brothers applied to the authorities for the release from customs of 'one case containing Oriental goods and some fancy weapons as knives, daggers, etc.'.[18] The application states the firm's intention to sell these wares at its shop, which suggests that it had been doing business in Malta for some time—enough time for it to have graduated from peddling to running an actual shop, at any rate. Be that as it may, by the first decade of the twentieth century there were at least ten Sindhwork firms in Malta, most of which had other branches elsewhere, including in the Far East, in the harbour towns around the Mediterranean, in east and west Africa, and in South America. The main trade appears to have been the export of silk and curios from the Far East and India, respectively, to the tourist and traveller crossroads of the Mediterranean and South America. There were also circuits of trade within the Mediterranean itself: for instance, in 1916, one Ramchand Kilumal applied for permission to export to Salonika (Thessaloniki in Greece) £25 worth of silver filigree, £50 worth of 'artificial silk goods', £50 worth of Maltese lace, £25 worth of 'fancy' embroidery, £10 worth of curios, and £50 in cash, the declared intention being to set up a shop in Salonika itself.[19]

The typical Sindhwork establishment in Malta was an import/export business and one or more shops in the port city and capital, Valletta. It is worth emphasizing that, to Sindhworkis, the sole attraction of Malta was its privileged place in the cartography of the British empire. Especially after the opening of the Suez Canal, most shipping routes through the Mediterranean included Malta in their itinerary. Valletta, the maritime city par excellence, saw a fast-flowing current of travellers, troops and the functionaries of the

British empire and their retinues. This was reflected in the spatial distribution of Sindhi businesses. The best shops were located on Strada Reale, still today the main social artery and shopping street in the city. There were secondary shops on the thoroughfares that connected Strada Reale to the harbour, and especially in places such as Ta' Liesse, where most travellers came ashore. Besides, Sindhis also routinely plied their trade from bumboats in the harbour itself. It is no exaggeration to say that from the time their ships dropped anchor to when they sailed, no traveller was ever too safely delivered from the temptations of the Sindhworkis' wares.

This location at one of the watering holes of the Empire was reflected in the kind of goods Sindhworkis sold. Until around 1930, their shops in Malta were mostly engaged in the curio and textiles trades. A 1907 photograph shows a typical shop sign that reads, 'Grand Indo-Egyptian Persian Bazaar, Suppliers to the German Imperial Family'. It was a message that was lapped up by travellers eager for their first taste of the orient—and, to a lesser extent, by locals who were after something exotic. (Things like kimonos and Satsuma ware found a ready market among à la mode Maltese.) Surviving records and inventories tell of Sindhwork shops that were stocked with all manner of Japanese ceramics, antimony, brassware, silks, silver filigree and embroidered cloth. Contemporary photographs suggest well-appointed shops with considerable attention to display. The firms themselves seem to have been well organized: all their correspondence was carried out on professionally printed letterheaded paper, and they often hired the services of the town's more established lawyers, especially when dealing with the colonial government. Invariably, the head offices were in Hyderabad, where the important organizational decisions regarding the firms were made and personnel recruited through kin and social networks.

Most of the Sindhworkis present in Malta at the time were agents on commission or salaried employees. Each firm had a manager, himself an agent of an owner, and a number of shop assistants who often doubled as cooks and servants, depending on its size. The owners of the larger firms are recorded as staying in Malta from time to time, presumably to check on the running of the branch and scout for new ideas and markets. During their period of employment in Malta, agents and employees lived together in housing provided by the firms, usually in Valletta itself or its suburb, Floriana. There was no question of them being joined by their wives or other members of their families who were not employees. The records show several instances where relatives worked together in the same firm: one Metharam Kirpalani, for instance, worked with his brother-in-law Thanvardas Nanumal, the proprietor of the firm N. Ramsami; Khushir Tahilram, son of Tahilram Thanvardas of Tahilram & Sons, worked in Malta for at least a year in 1915; in 1919, Parmanand Udhavadas petitioned for his nephew to be allowed to travel to Malta in order to manage business affairs; Ramchand Kilumal, of Ramchand & Thanvardas, was in joint business with his brother Gopaldas Kilumal.[20]

It would seem that sometime in the 1930s, Sindhwork firms in Malta experienced a sharp drop in profits due to the direct and indirect effects of global recession. The silk and curio markets in particular were heavily hit, and firms like Udhavadas & Co. went under entirely.[21] In at least some of the cases, the business was taken over by former employees who were ready to operate at lower margins, so much so that most of the Sindhi families in Malta today are the descendants of those employees. While the curio and novelties trade did not entirely die out, there was a shift away from it and in the direction of textiles trade for the local market. By the 1940s, the mainstay of Sindhi business in Malta had become the import, wholesale and retail of textiles for Maltese consumers. More on that later, but it was a shift that was evident elsewhere, and had much to do with the successful transition of Sindhwork away from the curio market.

The biography of Kishinchand Chellaram, as pieced together by the Sindhi writer Kavita Daswani, gives us a personalized sense of this spirit of enterprise and growth. In truth, Chellaram was not the average businessman. Together with the firms Choitram and Chanrai, the firm he set up enjoyed a reputation among Sindhis as one of the 'three Cs', arguably the three most prominent Sindhwork firms of the twentieth century. Chellaram was born Harkishin Chellaram Daryanani in Hyderabad in 1880. His father, Chellaram Gianchand, worked far away from home in Madras, as an itinerant trader at first but eventually running his own shops selling textiles, curios and carpets. At fifteen, Kishinchand joined his father in Madras, as did his three younger brothers in due course, and the family business soon expanded to Ooty (today Udhagamandalam), which at the time was a favourite destination of the British—as well as of Sindhworkis. In 1916, Kishinchand left his father's business and set up his own company, K. Chellaram, with a pedhi in Hyderabad in Shahi Bazaar where many of the Sindhwork firms were based. Madras was his, or rather his agents', first destination, where his firm traded in cotton and, more notably, in luxury goods such as silk, brocades, ivory, silver, brassware and carpets. In 1917, K. Chellaram set up a branch in Bombay specializing in wholesale trading in Japanese and Chinese silk. This was followed by three more shops in Madras (including one which was devoted exclusively to Kanchipuram silk) and, in 1918, in Ooty. At about the same time, Chellaram also expanded his business in the Kalbadevi neighbourhood of Bombay, where he was one of the founders of the Sind Work Merchants Association and the Silk Merchants Association. His first foray outside of India was to Yokohama, from where his agents exported Japanese textiles to Bombay and imported Indian-made goods, often to and from the Indian branches of the firm itself. In 1920, Kishinchand dispatched his son Tahilram to Gibraltar. Sons and agents were hived off to branch after new branch, and by 1930, the firm ran import, export, retail or wholesale operations in Bombay, Madras, Coimbatore, Hyderabad (in the Deccan), Secunderabad, Calcutta, Benares, Delhi and Ahmedabad in India, and also in New York, London,

Melilla, Hamburg, Milan, Gibraltar, Tangier, Kobe, Hong Kong, Shanghai, Colombo, Singapore, Jakarta and Nigeria. By 1938, there were branches in the Gold Coast, Sierra Leone and Gambia. The case of Nigeria gives us a fascinating glimpse into how Sindhwork businesses grew:

> Kishinchand had established a presence in Nigeria, under the name Kishinchand Chellaram & Sons, during the early 1920s, when J.T. Chanrai was already part of the local landscape. Originally, the branch was in the form of a warehouse used to store imported sundry goods which were distributed to wholesalers throughout the country. His third son, Asandas was a good friend of Tulsidas Chanrai, who was married to Kishinchand's sister, Kimatbai. Asandas was a convivial, gregarious man who enjoyed socialising and in the course of an evening out with Tulsidas, he enquired as to where J.T. Chanrai's large volumes of Madras cotton handloom textiles were being shipped. He had always assumed the bales were destined for England, based on the details listed on the company's bills of landing. Tulsidas revealed that the goods were being trans-shipped through Liverpool, but were actually headed for Nigeria. Demand was strong, and the quantities being shipped were huge. Asandas relayed this information to Kishinchand, who immediately hired a manager, Bhagomal Daryanani, gave him a 30 per cent partnership and packed him off to Nigeria.[22]

The story lends much support to the thesis that Sindhwork was a network in the proper sense of the word. As Markovits puts it, 'Sindhwork firms constituted a network both economically and socially, because they all traded in the same kind of goods, using the same commercial techniques, sharing information and recruiting staff from the same local pool of labour. The unity of the network came from its extreme centralization in Hyderabad.'[23] The growth model worked, because at the time of his death in 1951, Kishinchand Chellaram's company had become the largest Sindhwork firm in the world. The two groups that resulted from the business split in the early seventies are still major players in a number of fields, including shipping, trade and manufacture.

In the adventure that was Sindhwork, mobility and innovation were inseparable. As the Sindhworkis travelled, their wares became more and more diverse. That said, the market template originally established by Sindhwork proper, so to say, continued to structure trade for a long time. In many ways, the curio and souvenir trade, which has provided so much employment and profit to Sindhis over the years, is a descendant of the original lines. But what exactly were Sindhworks?

The collections of the Victoria and Albert Museum (V&A) give us some idea: a set of wooden chess pieces made in Thatta in 1867, turned on a *kharad* lathe and finely lacquered; a plate made in Thatta in 1880, in earthenware, with a black painted ornament over a white slip; a red silk handkerchief from 1867; and several contemporary tunics and shirts in silk and richly embroidered cotton. In the seventeenth and eighteenth centuries, the major manufacturing centre of Sindh appears to have been the town of Thatta, which was

particularly well known for its glazed pottery. By the
nineteenth century, the bulk of production had shifted
to Hyderabad, and to a lesser extent, to the small
town of Hala. Of particular note was Hala pottery:
tiles, dishes, vases and flower pots, typically glazed
in turquoise, dark purple, green or brown, and often
decorated with flower motifs. Arms, and notably the
enamelled matchlocks, shields and sabres that the Mirs
were so fond of, were produced in a number of places
in Sindh. There was leatherware, too, and textiles such
as silk lungis embroidered in gold and silver. Carpets
and ornamental silks and cottons were manufactured in
small quantities in Hyderabad, Sehwan and Shikarpur.
Just as famous as Hala pottery was a regional tradition
of lacquered woodwork, which used local woods that
were etched or painted with flower motifs, hunting
scenes and such. The objects made included boxes,
map and pen holders, flower stands and, as we know
from the V&A museum- chess sets.[24]

The benefit of hindsight helps us understand
that Sindh in the mid-nineteenth century had all
the ingredients for success. Here was a region with a
tradition of quality artisanal production, which had
just found itself embedded in an expanding global
market at a time when artisanware was the thing to
buy—especially if it came with a reputation. Certainly,
Sindhwork enjoyed that: as early as 1636, an English
agent reported to the East India Company that 'for
all Indian goods none are in such request as those of

Synda nor finde more reddie vend as being in regaarde of their substance and coullers most requirable'.[25]

However, it was only in the nineteenth century that that reputation started to really travel well, and over long distances. In 1843, for example, Postans noted that articles of Hyderabad lacquered woodwork were 'esteemed as great curiosities even in England'.[26] In the first Industrial Exhibition ever held in Sindh, which opened in Karachi in 1869, the carpets of Shikarpur, the embroideries and lacquered wares of Hyderabad, and the pottery of Hala were given pride of place, and the Hala artisans won several prizes for the quality of their goods.[27] Meanwhile, in far-off England, the catalogue for the London International Exhibition of 1871 spoke highly of the pottery of Hala as a paragon of Sindhi art.[28] The case of the London Exhibition is telling, because this was a time of considerable European and British nostalgia for the 'authentic' crafts of societies imagined as pre-industrial.[29] The market for Sindhwork was in part the product of new ideas about manufacture, and a corresponding shift in European taste and demand. By the 1860s, the traders of Hyderabad found that there was a growing global appetite for the wares that had previously found favour within the narrow confines of the Talpur court, local elites and the occasional traveller. The new routes proved highly productive, well-trodden as they were by British and European travellers eager to acquire objects of 'oriental' artisanal manufacture. Those were also the days of a developing tourist trade, and tourists, then as now, were keen to take home souvenirs from their travels.

This, then, was Sindhwork in the original and pure sense of the word. For various reasons, it was a term that would soon undergo considerable inflation. The evidence suggests that the renaissance in artisanal manufacture that took place in Sindh immediately after its annexation by the British did not last more than a couple of decades. Before long, and while still known generically as Sindhworkis, the traders of Hyderabad were dealing in a number of lines that had little to do with the pottery of Hala or the carpets of Shikarpur. Two in particular stand out: textiles\ and curios. As we have seen, Sindh as a region had a long tradition of quality textile production and trade. It was, however, the Hyderabadi Sindhworkis who first involved themselves in the large-scale and long-distance trade in textiles (silk, mainly) between the Far East, India and the West. Although Sindhis were dealing in silk in places such as Shanghai as early as the mid-nineteenth century, their business took off when they discovered that Japan was a source of good-quality and affordable silk. When Yokohama, which was soon to be the hub of the Japanese silk trade, opened its ports in the 1880s, Sindhis were quick to establish business there. By that time, Japan had become a world leader in the production of silk. The price of Japanese silk was as much as half that of the competition, and its quality and colour were considered superior. For a number of reasons, the Japanese relied for the export of their product, on foreign merchants and their trade networks.

Sindhwork firms such as Wassiamal set up branches in Yokohama, from where they exported the product—to India, mainly, but also to places such as west Africa. By the end of the Meiji period (1868–1912), a substantial portion of the Japanese silk trade was in fact controlled by the Sindhworkis of Yokohama.[30]

And yet, once again, the Sindhwork diaspora refuses to lend itself to a purely localized reading. In fact, nothing demonstrates this better than the silk trade. The growth of the Japanese market—together with that of the Chinese market, which was by no means insignificant—spawned a network that went well beyond Yokohama or Shanghai. Thus, in the early twentieth century, a Sindwork Silk Merchants Association was set up in Bombay, where much of the import trade into India was centred. In Ceylon, so vigorous was the involvement of Sindhworkis in the silk trade that litigation often broke out between them and the indigenous traders over matters like employment practices.[31] In Malta, Sindhwork shops advertised and sold different types of silk such as crêpe de Chine, Japanese diaphanous and *habutai* silk, and products such as Japanese kimonos, silk shawls and scarves. Many of these shops were run by firms that had branches/depots in Japan and China, thus securing the benefits of in-house trade.

With respect to curios, the line is more difficult to pin down. In the case of Sindhwork, curios were objects that had one or both of two characteristics: they were of, or evoked the 'orient', and they enjoyed a wide reputation for quality and authenticity associated with some or other region of origin. As Sindhis travelled, they encountered more and more of these objects. A fine example is that of Maltese lace. It is almost certain that Sindhworkis had little knowledge of it when they first arrived in Malta. The local lace industry, however, rose in profile during the latter half of the nineteenth century, through the various international exhibitions and the much-publicized patronage of Queen Victoria. This created and fuelled an international demand, and it is estimated that by the turn of the century up to 7,000 Maltese women were involved in the cottage manufacture of lace. The Sindhworkis saw their chance. The firms stocked their shops in Malta with the lace, and more impressively, tapped into their global networks to export substantial quantities of it to north Africa, Batavia (today Jakarta) and Johannesburg, among other places. By the first years of the twentieth century, most Sindhwork firms in Malta had positioned themselves as commission agents and retailers, and in some cases even subcontractors, for the manufacture of Maltese lace. Thus, the entrepreneurial potency of the typical Sindhworki firm—with a head office in Hyderabad and various agents in other places who were always on the lookout for markets. What's more, the firms did not just come across markets ready-made: at times, they actively created and cultivated them. One of the Sindhworki sources I sat with showed me a prize that had been awarded to his grandfather's firm (J.T. Chanrai, one of the major Sindhwork players) for 'exhibiting and promoting gift objects' and curios in Buenos Aires.

Precisely because it was so perennially innovative, it is hard to contain and classify the Sindhwork trade. In Malta, for example, the list of wares advertised by Sindhi firms at the turn of the twentieth century includes ornamental firearms, gold and silver filigree work, 'Indian, Chinese, Japanese, Persian and Egyptian Art Curiosities', Japanese Damascene wares such as cigarette cases, brooches, small boxes and vases, Indian silver tea-sets, carpets, Indian brassware and enamelled metal ornaments, 'oriental' jewellery, 'Tenerife hand-drawn threadwork' (another example of a product encountered en route the journey of the diaspora), and Japanese antimony and porcelain wares. In Sierra Leone, the early Sindhworkis sold Madras kerchiefs, imported through branches in Cape Town, Gibraltar and Las Palmas.[32] In 1918, Kishinchand Chellaram's first shop in the British Indian hill resort of Ooty sold woollen and silk clothing, textiles, brassware, silver figurines and even French perfumes.[33] Perhaps the one class that comes up again and again is that of Japanese goods, prominently advertised as such. No surprise there, because the late nineteenth century was the heyday of *japonisme*—the craze about everything Japanese, which saw a deluge of fans, ceramics, enamelwares, masks, screens, kimonos and a hundred other things pour enchantment into homes, especially in Europe and North America.

In sum, and contrary to its apparently restrictive name, Sindhwork was very much about diversification. The trend continued into the twentieth century, wherever Sindhis did business. In Japan, for example, cotton and other newer types of textiles replaced

silk as the major export commodity in the 1930s.[34]
Advertisements from Sierra Leone show that by 1939
Sindhi firms had begun to import 'general items'
from Britain and continental Europe.[35] In many
cases, Sindhworkis realized that, profitable as it may
have been, the curio and souvenir trade was limited
and often fickle. (It took a big hit during the Great
Depression, for example.) There was a gradual shift
towards the utility sectors: textiles for everyday use,
household items, foodstuffs and such. Once again
the Sindhi firms, with their deep-rooted infrastructure
of global networks and knowledge, were well equipped
to make the change.

The Organization of Sindhi Global Trade

One of my first Sindhi sources of knowledge about
the community in Malta was Kishore, who was then
in his nineties. Born in Hyderabad just before the
First World War, he had been a trader all his working
life, had travelled and lived in four continents and
had established a Sindhwork business with trading
connections in fifteen countries. As we talked, we
were surrounded by a lively troupe of his great-
grandchildren. For all his 'navy' tattoos and the glint of
the adventurer-trader in his eyes, something had kept
this man's life together as an individual, as a member of
a community and a family. It is not unreasonable to ask
how Sindhworkis managed to keep their social fabric
intact even as they constantly moved around in search
of trading opportunities.

Until Partition, Sindhwork was a trade diaspora with a single, clear centre. The traders may have spent much of their lives abroad as agents or employees of the firms, or simply as itinerant traders, but it was to Hyderabad that their homing instincts took them. In many ways, the town was the social and commercial heart of the diaspora, and many Sindhwork firms were based in the Shahi bazaar neighbourhood. A case in point was Kishinchand Chellaram, whose 'entire global network of close to 100 main branches, warehouses, offices and tiny outlets under the Kishinchand Chellaram umbrella was being guided by one quiet and withdrawn man who treasured the simplicity and sameness of his life in a pedhi in Hyderabad'.[36] It would appear that while the Sindhwork bosses did sometimes travel between their various branches and depots, they were likely to spend more and more time sedentary in Hyderabad as their businesses grew. Delegation—to sons, in-laws, managers and agents—made it possible for them to sit in their pedhis and focus on the more strategic aspects of their trade.

Away from the pedhis, Hyderabad—more specifically, the district of Hirabad—was also the heart of social life for the Sindhworki bhaibands. One popular spot was the Bhaiband Club, a Victorian gentlemen's club with a bar, billiard tables, lounges and a dining area. Sindhworkis, and particularly the wealthier owners of the more established firms, would often spend their evenings socializing at the club. Hyderabad also had a Rotary Club and at least one Masonic Lodge. (A few affluent Sindhworkis, and probably some influential and Anglophile amils, were Freemasons.) Marcus Banks has described how, in the Gujarati town of Jamnagar, the places where mobile Jain traders socialized were the start of many a trade adventure; word would get around that business in, say, Africa was good, and travel plans would be made.[37] Which is not to say that in Jamnagar, or in Hyderabad, traders shared information openly, out of love for their fellow men: on the contrary, the evidence suggests that there was intense competition between their firms. The point is that Hyderabad functioned as the centre of the trade diaspora also in the sense that it was the place where the journeys and profits of business were at their most conspicuous, and where aspirations were fuelled and connections made. Certainly, as Sindhwork gained traction and profits grew, the havelis of the more affluent merchant families got more and more opulent, prominent and appetizing. A number of them survive in Hyderabad today, testimony to the main chance that birthed Sindhwork.

It was not just the men who, intentionally or not, circulated information and made connections. Although the Sindhi women were generally not directly involved in trade, they had, through proximity to their male kin and social circles, a considerable knowledge of business practices. Hyderabad was ultimately a small town, and Hirabad was even smaller. It was and still is a practice among Hindu Sindhi women to recite morning prayers and the Sukhmani Sahib path at the local Nanakpanth tikana. There was no shortage of opportunities for them to socialize and compare notes on, for example, who was travelling where. Here it ought to be pointed out that until Partition, the women of the Sindhworki families stayed behind in Hyderabad while their men travelled. The mobility of the men notwithstanding, a woman was still part of a functional patrilocal joint family living under one roof and eating from the same kitchen. This kinship structure was reflected in the layout of especially the larger havelis in Hyderabad: it typically consisted of a central courtyard with rooms on the upper floors for the various couples and their children, and common rooms and servants' quarters on the ground floor.

Hyderabad was also the place where the people of the diaspora were recruited. Sindhworkis were for the most part Hyderabadi bhaibands, although members of other groups—bhatias, amils, and bhaibands who were not from Hyderabad—were sometimes taken on as employees at the firms. To be a Hyderabadi bhaiband was a resource or, as a sociologist might put it, social capital, in the sense that the group perceived itself as, and indeed was well placed to be, adept at Sindhwork. Hyderabadi bhaibands had the collective experience of the community at their disposal—they could rely on networks of trust and credit, and their families formed knowledge bases in the neighbourhoods where they lived. There were two means by which people were recruited. The first was through kinship links: a Sindhworki boss looking to broaden his network or explore a new market would appoint his sons, or take on relatives, as employees or agents. The second means was through a fabric of patronage within the bhaiband community in Hyderabad. The owners of the larger businesses were under constant pressure to provide employment in their firms to young men known to them or their families socially in Hyderabad. It was common for people, both men and women, to petition for employment on behalf of sons or other family members.

With respect to employment itself, one system was based on the old shah-gumashta arrangement described by Seth Naomul, in which the owner of the firm (the shah) employed agents and working partners (the gumashtas) to run the various branches. Agents could work on a commission basis and thus enjoy some degree of autonomy and possibly some business on the side. The other, and over time, the more frequently used system was that of salaried employees, normally recruited on three-year formal contracts that bound both employer and employee for the duration of that period. Bhaiband boys were enrolled at a young age (fifteen or so was a typical age for a son, slightly older for a relative or acquaintance) and assigned to a branch.

Life as an employee of a Sindhwork firm was not necessarily a day at the beach. The men were usually housed in basic quarters, although senior employees often had separate rooms. The working hours were long, typically twelve to fifteen hours a day with half a day off on Sundays—and even this was not guaranteed, if records of litigations from Malta are anything to go by. A particularly fascinating case is that of one Nathermal Moolchand, who in 1904 secured a three-year contract (through an uncle in Hyderabad) as a 'cook and pedlar' with the firm Neechamal Teumal. The terms were that Nathermal would stay in Malta for the duration of the contract, and that the passage from and to Hyderabad would be paid for by his employer. But things did not go as planned. Eighteen months after his arrival in Malta, the firm sacked Nathermal, accusing him of being 'drunk and quarrelsome'. Left without the means to go back home, and quite destitute, Nathermal petitioned the British authorities in Malta to fund his passage back to Hyderabad. The petition, written on his behalf by a gentleman named Rughumal Rupchand in Hyderabad, goes like this:

It is a well known fact here, even the local papers decry these SindhWork merchants as notoriously cruel and a regular source of harrassment for their servants, whose services they secure with great inducements and promises, which they honour more in breach than in fulfilment. Such is the effect of the shabby treatment that the employees receive, that once they have served them for the time agreed upon, they would not even for a mint of money, go back to their employment. Neechamal's firm had Nathermal Moolchand in their employ for 18 months, during which they paid half the salary to his mother every month, the remaining to be paid by the firm, which they are bound by the agreement to pay, but they refuse to render it to Nathermal without any justifying cause . . . The above named servant is a native Indian subject of His Majesty King Emperor and is a resident of Hyderabad Sindh in Bombay Presidency.[38]

This was probably something of an exceptional case, but people who were employed with the firms in the mid-twentieth century recall that rather than a job in the nine-to-five sense, Sindhwork was an all-embracing way of life. Workers were expected to be at the service of their managers round the clock: one employee said he was expected to massage his manager's feet at the end of the day's work, and another described how his manager would routinely rob him of his few free hours on Sunday to help him deal with the correspondence. Various harsh words—'exploitation', 'bloodsuckers', 'slavery' and the like were used by my sources to describe their conditions or their managers at work. The evidence suggests that as Sindhwork mushroomed and became more structured, the gap between employers and employees, the 'bosses' and those 'in service', widened, and drifted away from the shah-gumashta model. The bosses had business experience, access to capital and credit, established networks of patronage and all the trappings of prestige and affluence. The employees, on the other hand, endured the routine of hard work, the only advantage of which was the hope of accumulating enough capital and experience to be able to set up their own business. Although 'bhaiband' literally means 'brotherhood', this was kinship of the lopsided variety. If employers and employees were brothers at all, they were very much on unequal terms.

By the mid-twentieth century, trading associations were being formed by Sindhis in Hong Kong, Singapore, Japan and many other places around the world. They were usually intended to protect their collective interests as local groups. At the same time, individual firms could be highly territorial. They expected complete loyalty from their employees, in some cases going so far as to discourage them from socializing with workers of other firms. If the staff of a firm slept under the same roof, ate and worked and did puja together, there was less risk of business intelligence leaking to other Sindhwork firms. A favourite story of older Sindhis tells of how an employee at a Sindhwork firm was instructed by his manager to take up stamp collecting. Or, rather, to pretend to do so—the idea being that any stamps passed on to the employee by employees of other firms could be used to piece together trails of business connections.

4. AN ENDURING LEGACY

By the time of Partition, Sindhwork had become a global trade diaspora. While still fuelled by mobility and entrepreneurship, it was far removed from the world of Hindu Sindhi traders of a hundred years earlier. First, its cartography had been redrawn. It was no longer restricted to the Arabian Sea or central Asia, as it had been for Seth Naomul and the Shikarpuri bankers, but was rather a truly global diaspora. Second, Sindhwork was also about the rise of formally structured and bureaucratically managed firms, as opposed to the earlier working partnerships. Third, the diaspora had changed from a network of shahs and gumashtas to one in which pockets of Sindhworkis, while still relating to Hyderabad as home, began to form trade associations and diversify in the various domestic markets they operated in. In a number of places, that diversification included industrial manufacture and hotels, among other things.

This raises the question as to whether or not we can speak of such a thing as Sindhwork in the mid-to-late twentieth century—or today, for that

matter. On the one hand, it might make sense to
limit the use of the word to the tight-knit network of
bhaiband traders centred in Hyderabad that thrived
between the 1860s and Partition. On the other,
however, for a number of reasons, this would be
unnecessary, and quite inaccurate. Certainly, Sindhis
themselves still use the word even in the context
of the present. Partly this is due to their family
histories and legacies. A family business known to be
descended from Sindhwork will often still be called
a Sindhwork business, notwithstanding its apparent
dissimilarity to its original pursuit. Second, and
perhaps more importantly, Sindhwork set the template
for a way of conducting business that is alive and well
among Sindhis around the world today—indeed, this
template is one of the features that defines them as a
group. It is a model that privileges mobility, the restless
exploration of new markets, and the tendency to tap
into family and ethnic resources as one of the means
to grow one's business. It was this model that inspired
and structured a large number of Sindhi businesses,
many of which were spawned after Partition in
families that did not have a tradition of Sindhwork.
There is one qualifier. While used pliably, the term
tends to be restricted to businesses based in places
that had a significant Sindhwork presence before
Partition. Given the geographical promiscuity of old-
school Sindhwork, this may not seem like much of
a restriction. It does, however, matter in places like
Dubai. Sindhis in Dubai are unlikely to be generically

called Sindhworkis, unless they are obviously
descended from old Sindhworki families.

At Partition, and like most other Hindu Sindhis,
the Sindhworkis moved with their families out of
Hyderabad and settled more or less permanently in
their various countries of operation. At the risk of
peddling counterfactual history, I would like to think
that if the Sindhwork diaspora had not happened,
Sindhis today would be based in India and in the
post-1947 destination countries such as Canada, the
UK and the Gulf states. In this respect, what matters
about Sindhwork is that it had, by the time of Partition,
put into place a well-established and thriving global
network of firms. It was a legacy that would have a
profound impact on the geography of Sindhi settlement.
This is also because after Partition, Sindhwork continued
to siphon young Sindhi men out of India, as it had done
from Hyderabad for several decades before Partition.

To some degree, the process is ongoing, and
exemplified by the experience of Bombay. After
Partition, the manpower of the Sindhwork firms was
kept nourished by bhaibands, and to a lesser extent by
Sindhis from other backgrounds who were now settled
in the city and whose families had found themselves
dispossessed of their traditional occupation of small-
time business in Sindh. This happened in two ways.
First, large global Sindhwork firms such as J.T.
Chanrai, K. Chellaram, and T. Choitram (the 'Three
Cs'), all of which had offices in Bombay, served up
recruitment possibilities for men who were willing
to join as salaried employees, and in the process

to leave India in search of opportunity elsewhere. Second, the inevitable splintering of Sindhwork firms worldwide, itself fuelled in part by former employees setting up on their own, meant that new businesses continued to mushroom all over the world. These new ventures called for more and more human resources, and the first resource for them was usually other Sindhis. No matter what their size or age, the firms preferred to employ young Sindhi men from India, as opposed to non-Sindhi locals in the places where they operated. It was common for family members or their friends and acquaintances to be recruited informally for these businesses through their connections in Bombay.

In practice, this was not always easy. A law passed in Gibraltar in 1923, for example, limited Indians and other aliens to one place of business for each licence holder. What's worse for the Sindhi businessmen- the number of alien employees was limited to what was deemed strictly necessary to run the business. In 1934, the Trade Restrictions Ordinance fixed the number of Indians that could own businesses in the colony at the grand figure of ten, and restricted their trade to 'oriental goods'. To Sindhwork and its spirit of expansion and enterprise, this was sacrilege, and called for some redemptive action. It turned out that a Sindhi business could actually grow and recruit, as long as it was in partnership with a local who held at least 60 per cent of the venture. So, a number of Sindhis did just that, and found local Christian or Jewish partners. Between 1934 and 1936 alone, this piece of lateral thinking resulted in no less than twelve new shops. Today, many Sindhi-owned shops in Gibraltar still carry the names of those partners: Márquez, Carlos, Antonio, and the like.

Nor was it just recruitment that was impacted by the new regulations. Until the implementation in 1983 of the British Nationality Act of 1981, restrictions on immigration meant that spouses were not awarded permanent residency, the fear being that the children born to these immigrants in Gibraltar would automatically qualify for British citizenship. The Sindhworkis' functional, if imperfect solution was for the men to live in Gibraltar and for the women and children to live in neighbouring Spain or Morocco. So rigid was the regime that immigrant women on monthly residence permits in Gibraltar who were found to be pregnant were immediately sent away.[1] The point cannot be overemphasized that it was not just opportunities and markets that Sindhis encountered in their various destinations. They also found themselves caught up in legal and other regulatory regimes that at times threatened to scupper those very opportunities. So the successful Sindhworki was also someone who was imaginative enough to circumvent those regimes.

But many of the new employees still eventually set up their own businesses, and the process snowballed. This, then, is how the large communities of Sindhis in places like Hong Kong and Nigeria developed. They are built on the foundations laid by the old Sindhwork firms, but they are also the result of post-Partition recruitment, enterprise and the perennial spirit of independence of the community. Sindhis themselves had such things to say: 'Most of the Indian shops had Indians working for them. But then, they had their own idea and would set up their own business'; 'I opened my own business; I had knowledge as well as contacts, which I got when working for a Sindhi importer'; 'There is the fact that contracts usually are on a three-year basis. After two or three terms, the boy makes money and decides to do some trade for himself. No one will give a newcomer credit except his former employer, who in so doing earns himself both a competitor as well as a customer. And the boy starts out on his own.' Writing about Sindhis in Hong Kong, Vaid noted this process: 'Generally speaking, after 2 or 3 such trips, the employee quits his employment to start his own mail order business.'[2]

This process of recruitment into Sindhwork is nowhere near as thriving today as it was in the first two or three decades following Partition. That said, Sindhwork—or rather, the kind of business that is its direct legacy—is still an option for young Sindhi men in Mumbai, and in India more generally. The main attraction is that it offers enterprising Sindhis the opportunity to travel, learn the ropes of trade and establish their reputation (and thus creditworthiness, among other things) within the global Sindhi business network. Even if Sindhwork recruitment and employment can be paternalistic and sometimes verge on the exploitative, the prospects they hold out are often deemed much more promising than those obtaining from the average job in India. Clearly, prospects are just that. Take Lal, who was thirty when I interviewed him in 2001. He comes from an amil family, but his education is little more than basic. He told me that ever since he was young he had dreamed of working abroad; as he grew older this wish had become more compelling, even as it dawned on him that wages in India for someone with his qualifications would never translate into riches. In 1990, at nineteen, he left India to go to Freetown in Sierra Leone on a two-and-a-half-year contract with a big Sindhwork firm. The contact was made through a family friend. When his contract expired, he left the firm and got a job as a clerk in Bombay. When we last spoke in 2001, he was trying to get his hands on a fresh contract with a Sindhwork firm. A couple of years before this, a well-connected Sindhworki amil who was known to the family had offered him a job in Curaçao. This however, had not worked out because of visa problems.

This, then, is the general picture. Through their periodic presence in Mumbai and through their families and friends, Sindhi 'bosses' (meaning anyone who runs a firm, be it a relatively small affair or a global business) present job opportunities for Sindhi men, generally those from less well-to-do families and lacking the kind of education that would secure them a good job in India. Even if diminished in scale compared to thirty or forty years ago, Sindhwork still acts as a stepping-stone for young Sindhis, a route to the world of mobile trade. Many Sindhis in self-employed business around the world today started out as employees of Sindhwork firms, where they learned not merely how to trade, but also how to conduct a particular type of trade based on mobility, how to set up wide-ranging business networks and develop a readiness to explore new markets and possibilities. At the same time, it must be said that over the years, Sindhi firms have shown themselves more and more willing to employ non-Sindhis, generally based on their formal qualifications and proven records, in their various countries of operation. This decreasing reliance on community-enrolled labour prompted Markovits to suggest that the decentring of the community in relation to Hyderabad weakened the sense of network that characterized Sindhwork prior to Partition—although there remain, as he puts it, 'important linkages, and Sindhi businessmen in a given country will always prefer doing business with other Sindhis in other countries than with non-Sindhis'[3]. While I agree that Sindhwork today is much less of a tight-knit bhaiband network than it was when hiring took place in the pedhis and clubs of Hyderabad, I do not think that the potential for Sindhi business worldwide to employing Sindhi labour is to be entirely discounted.

Readiness to Diversify

The many organizational changes within Sindhwork went hand in hand with tremendous diversification. While a good number of Sindhi shops and businesses today deal in articles that could creatively trace their genealogy to 'the work of Sindh'—Indian handicrafts, textiles and so on—many others do not. Sindhwork may be a cherished legacy among Sindhis, but certainly not to the extent that it traps them in a nostalgic conservatism. So diverse is Sindhi business today that it is probably worth making the point through examples.

The Malta Sindhi story serves as well as any other, and is our first example. As we have seen, from the late 1930s onwards, Sindhi businesses in Malta were mostly in the hands of the former agents of the Sindhwork firms who had become the owners of the retail outlets set up by these firms. Apart from the families of the traders who moved from Hyderabad to Malta (often via a number of intermediate stops in India or elsewhere) to join their menfolk permanently, no significant influx of Sindhis, along the model of new recruitments from India resulting from the splintering of major firms, happened after Partition. There were two reasons for this. First, Malta being a small island with limited market possibilities, it was not seen as a land of opportunity, as were places such as Hong Kong and Singapore. Second, from 1952 to 1985, the country's tight immigration laws meant that the only way a Sindhi man could apply for residency in the country was by marrying a local woman. As Tikam complained to me, 'We wanted to do favours to our cousins, but we couldn't. In 1952, the doors were closed and we couldn't bring anyone to Malta. For thirty-three years not a single person came from India.' The upshot is that Sindhi businesses in Malta have tended to be passed down among a handful of families, who have otherwise remained socially and commercially well-connected to Sindhis across the world. In 1955, Sindhi traders in Malta came together to set up the Indian Merchants'

Association (Malta). The Association was never particularly active, and in 1989, it was renamed the Maltese-Indian Community, an organization which was less concerned with trade than it was with the running of the Sindhi mandir and community cultural events.

By the onset of the Second World War, the strength of Sindhi business in Malta had become the import, wholesale and retail of textiles, mainly for the local market. Many of the shops that had originally specialized in curios and luxury goods shifted towards and diversified into textiles for women's clothing. This proved a wise choice. The post-War period in Malta was one of growing affluence and social aspirations. The textiles sector gained steadily in importance as Maltese women at large (as opposed to a small urban elite) became aware of fashion and started making and wearing clothes that went beyond the utilitarian, toying with style and material. In the period between the late 1950s and the mid-1970s, Sindhi retailers enjoyed a veritable bonanza of trade. Through their families and trading connections in the Far East, and notably Japan, they were well-placed to source affordable and good-quality textiles. They were also able to hold their own in the face of competition from Maltese businesses, to the extent that the saying among Maltese seamstresses was that if you wanted quality textiles, the place to find them was at the Indian shops in Valletta. (Since there were no other Indians in Malta, Sindhis were simply called '*l-Indjani*'- 'the Indians'). Besides, a number of

Sindhi shops specialized in high-quality textiles for weddings and other formal occasions.

Things were to change yet again, however. In the last quarter of the century, Malta's female workforce increased and diversified even as wage discrimination by gender was legally banned in 1976. This meant more women with less time and more cash to spare, who needed smart clothes for everyday use, and who were therefore likely to buy ready-mades. Sindhi businesses were quick to respond. By the mid-1980s, almost all the textile shops in Valletta had switched their line to ready-made clothing, with an emphasis on the lower-middle end of the market. Competition with Maltese-owned businesses was intense, but the Sindhis were able to combine competitive prices with good quality, and they managed to hold their ground in this new sector remarkably well. In fact, the proliferation of Maltese-owned boutiques offered new opportunities for Sindhis, since almost all of the latter doubled as wholesalers. Most boutiques owned and run by the Maltese were small ventures that depended on wholesalers with established import links for their stocks. The Sindhis tapped into their knowledge of markets and their long-established and far-reaching networks of trade to supply these small retailers.

That said, not all Sindhi businesses made the shift from curios to textiles to ready-mades. A few continued to operate in Sindhwork-type lines. The market was good, and included tourists as well as Maltese people looking for gifts or affordable home decorations. These bazaar-type shops were explorative and innovative in their choice of lines.

In the early 1980s, for instance, goods such as quartz watches and electronic calculators and games were all the rage. Once again, the Sindhis' connections in Hong Kong, Japan and the other industrial production centres of the Far East placed them in an excellent position to import, retail, and to wholesale to Maltese shopkeepers. Their shops, situated as they were on Malta's prime shopping run and stocked with the latest gadgets, were all but assured brisk business. Further, their location meant that they were ideally placed to milk another major boom, when it came. In the 1970s and 1980s, tourism grew dramatically from an insignificant trickle, and in 1989 the annual figure of 1 million was reached. A number of Sindhi businesses turned increasingly to selling souvenirs. In one shop, Malta-themed brass door-knockers, locally crafted glass, figurines in Maltese costume, and local craft pottery rubbed shoulders with wares that would not have been out of place in a Sindhwork shop in the early twentieth century: Indian-made leather horses, wooden carvings of Indian musicians in the Rajasthani style, animal figurines, leather sandals from India, Chinese ladies' fans, kimonos, incense sticks and a large collection of fishbone carvings.

From the 1970s, the Sindhis in Malta ventured increasingly into new lines and forms of organization. For example, one business set up in 1972 specialized in industrial supplies and employed a number of Maltese people. A number of Sindhis opened Indian restaurants, often as a side business to their main import and wholesale trade. They were staffed by chefs and waiters brought over especially from India (not Sindhis, though), and two restaurants were co-owned with Maltese partners. One entrepreneur, whose father was in the import, wholesale and retail of souvenirs and bazaar-type goods, set up a real estate agency, again in partnership with a Maltese businessman. The list of such ventures is long.

The second example which illustrates diversification concerns one of the best known and oldest established Sindhi business families. Throughout much of the twentieth century, the Chanrai firm occupied a secure place in the holy trinity of Sindhwork firms. Of the three, it is arguably Chanrai that weathered the years best and emerged as a firm with major assets, operations and interests in a large number of countries, notably in Africa and south-east Asia. One of the things that make Chanrai worth paying attention to is that it has not stuck to trade. Rather, it has been more than willing to strike out in industry, manufacturing and finance. We will again come across this particular incarnation of Sindhi adaptability in the next chapter: in Ulhasnagar, a city about 50 kms from Mumbai, a large number of Partition refugees took to cottage, and in some cases industrial and manufacturing.

The Chanrai family name was originally the distinctly more Sindhi-sounding Uttamchandani. As in the case of Chellaram (Daryanani, originally), the name Chanrai was first used for the business, and in due course came to be used as the family name. Already a wealthy Sindhworki family back in Sindh, the Chanrais lived as an extensive joint family in two large havelis in Hyderabad, on a street that actually bore the family name. Family oral history cites a Chanrai Uttamchand who traded in bullion and commodities (food, mostly) in Karachi, as the first ancestor of note. By the 1860s, two brothers, Jhamatmal and Thakurdas, had set up the firm J.T. Chanrai. Originally dealing in textiles in Sindh, it eventually expanded to include Sindhwork objects, with depots in Karachi and Bombay. The twist came sometime in the 1870s, when on one occasion the firm supplied goods on credit to a Sindhworki named Titu, who ran small-time business in Malta. It so happened that Titu went bankrupt and Chanrai, his creditors, sent over an agent to take over his concern. From then on, expansion was rapid: Malta led to Gibraltar, Sirte, Tangier, Ceuta, the Canary Islands, Sierra Leone, Ghana, Nigeria and, certainly by the start of the First World War, Argentina, Chile and Brazil. While at this time the expansion route was mostly limited to British-held territories, later expansion included places like (French-held, after the Ottoman collapse) Lebanon. In 1934, a branch established in Madras pioneered export of the well-known 'Madras check' handkerchief to west Africa, where it gained much popularity.

As the firm grew, it became more and more difficult to keep up the supply of Indian goods via export from Bombay. So the firm diversified, developing supply stations in Shanghai, Yokohama, Kobe, Osaka, Indonesia and Singapore, among other places. This growth also meant that the firm became one of the major employers for young Sindhi men, who would be recruited in India for the most part and posted in the various branches, shops and depots around the world. The years following Partition were particularly significant in this respect, even if non-Sindhi employment grew as the firm diversified into areas like industry, which required specially-trained human resources. What's more, a substantial number of Sindhi businesses in Nigeria today stem from the Chellaram and Chanrai companies. In this sense, the Chanrai firm is yet another example of how major Sindhwork firms often served as a fertile ground for enterprising individuals to gain a foothold in global business.

The Chanrai empire today is made of a number of branches and offshoots, the result of decades of (amicable, for the most part) business splits. Perhaps the most consequential split came about in 1948, when Kewalram Ghanshamdas (Thakurdas's grandson) formed a separate company, the Kewalram Chanrai Group. The firm's main operations were in India, Africa and the Far East, and it diversified into department stores, among other lines. From the 1960s, new ventures included an integrated textiles plant as well as extension farming to grow and gin cotton in Nigeria under its subsidiary companies, Afprint and Afcott, respectively. In 1975, another subsidiary, PT Kewalram Indonesia, set up a spinning and embroideries plant in Bandung; Kewalram Indonesia is now the main textiles division of the Group. In 1981, the Group acquired Kewalram Oils, a company that recycles palm residue in Malaysia. In 1989, Kewalram Philippines was set up to manufacture synthetic blended yarns. In 1989, Olam was established in Nigeria to set up a non-oil export operation. With its original headquarters in London, it started by exporting raw cashew nuts and then expanded into cotton, cocoa and shea nuts. The headquarters were moved to Singapore in 1996, and Olam is at present, a major company with operations worldwide. In the late twentieth century, the Group diversified into commercial property development in Singapore, Malaysia and USA. The Kewalram Chanrai Group has over the years been run by brothers working together: this, in the words of a family member I interviewed in London, has been one of the reasons behind its success. Today, the Group is worth billions of dollars, and members of the Chanrai family have inhabited the highest regions of Forbes wealth rankings. They have also been prominently involved in patronage of various charities and non-commercial/public service groups, notable examples being the Chinmaya Mission and the private Jaslok Hospital in Mumbai.

The third example takes us to Hong Kong, where the Harilela (Mirchandani, originally) family occupies a high perch among Sindhis. The opulence of their seventy-bedroom Mughal-style Kowloon mansion is the stuff of legend, and they inhabit a rarefied stratosphere as philanthropists, patrons and key players in business and high-society circles, generally. The first Halilela to venture outside of India was Lilaram, who left Hyderabad for Singapore in the early 1920s. Moving on to Guangzhou, he traded in the classical Sindhwork lines: ivory, jade and embroidered Chinese stoles, exporting to the United States, among other places. He eventually moved to Hong Kong, where his son Hari (1922–

2014) emerged as an astute businessman specializing in tailoring. In part, he owed his success to the relations he cultivated with British army officers, a friendship that brought him much dividend during the Second World War. A stream of contracts for military uniforms followed, on the back of which came a demand for civilian tailoring. One highly lucrative line was bespoke tailoring by mail order (the '24-hour suit', for which Hong Kong tailors are still renowned). At its height in the 1950s and 1960s, the Harilela business turned out hundreds of suits a day.[4] As is often the case with Sindhis, Harilela put his growing networks and assets to good use and diversified into real estate, restaurants, overseas trade and notably, hotels. Today, the Harilela Group owns and operates a number of luxury hotels around the world. They include The Hari and the InterContinental in Hong Kong, Holiday Inn hotels in Hong Kong, Bangkok, Changzhou, Singapore and Penang, the 50 Bowery in New York, and The Hari in London. The board of directors is entirely manned by members of the family, who together are worth a conservative estimate of hundreds of millions of dollars. Such an institution has the family become, that when Hari died in 2014, one of the visitors to the family home was Hong Kong Chief Executive Leung Chun-ying.

The last example is the story of Sindhis in Malaysia, where they (together with Gujaratis) have for a long time enjoyed a major presence in the textiles trade. The first Sindhis here were Sindhworkis who established themselves in the coastal towns in Malaya in the 1880s. It was however, Partition that really consolidated the

Sindhi presence here. While they remain preeminent in textiles, they do business in a number of fields, including real estate, electronics, department stores, entertainment, food and jewellery. The well-known Sindhis in Malaysia include the tycoon Rupchand Binwani, the owner of Binwani's fashion and textiles group, and Utamal Valiram.[5] First established as a textiles business in Kuala Lumpur in 1935, the Valiram business now operates 350 stores in south-east Asia representing over 200 luxury and hospitality brands.

Each of these businesses has its own particular biography, defined in part by local circumstances. From a trade diaspora centred on a tight-knit community based in Hyderabad, Sindhwork metamorphosed into a geographically dispersed, if networked, collection of local experiences. Expanding a business beyond one's immediate locality and country, employing people who then often set up their own businesses and in turn employing other people to perpetuate the cycle, exploring as many lines as possible in as many places as possible—these and other characteristics of Sindhwork are today true of a good chunk of Sindhi business worldwide. Today, the business activities of some of the most hallowed Sindhi names in the world, as well as those of the lesser-known names in the community, are by no means limited to trade. The well-trodden notion that Sindhis are a 'trading community' who will only venture into other fields if absolutely necessary, and then with much reluctance, is a myth.

5. SINDHI BUSINESS IN INDIA AFTER PARTITION

'Of all Partition migrants, the Sindhis have willed themselves to forget Partition most successfully. When you meet Sindhis, this forgetting does not come across as repressed memory, but as a pragmatic and mercantile decision to move ahead with life.'[1] This is how Rita Kothari, a scholar and herself a Sindhi, sums up the reluctance of Sindhis in India to engage with Partition as a traumatic event in their history. As she sees it, the hard-nosed pragmatism which helped Sindhi refugees weather the storm of Partition disallowed any narrative sentimentality. Besides, the very qualities that made Sindhis exemplary actors of Partition—their business acumen and 'cultural openness'—effectively robbed them of a leading role in a dominant Partition discourse that is founded on narratives of violence and rupture.

I think Kothari is largely right. As I listened to the stories of Sindhi settlement in India, their drift was that of business acumen and practical good sense prevailing over adversity, including the adversity of Partition. As I have argued, Partition is a defining event of contemporary Sindhi history and identity. It is not forgotten, but rather remembered in very specific ways. If the theme of trauma is brought up at all, it is never foregrounded: rather, it figures as a bump in the road towards success. This is a book about business, and it is not my task here to dive into the violent events of 1947–48 in the Indian subcontinent. Rather, I shall take up the narrative favoured by Sindhis themselves, to explore some of the ways in which they established themselves as a business community in India after Partition.

The storyline I came across again and again is simple enough, and goes as follows: back in Sindh, Hindus were a prosperous minority. Partition uprooted them forcibly and dispossessed them of their livelihood and assets. A period of business on the margins and, for many, of real economic hardship, followed. In time, this gave way to stability, success and, in some cases, great wealth and prestige. It is fundamentally a riches-to-rags-to-riches story, and one punctuated by the twin notions of hard work and business acumen. The subplot is that Sindhis pulled it off under their own steam, with little outside help from the state or anyone else. This explains the favourite assertion among Sindhis in India today that, no matter how desperate, a Sindhi will never beg. If stories of the violence of Partition are thin on the ground for the Sindhi community, the same cannot be said of the stories of their stoic self-reliance. Sindhis in India like to recount how, as refugees, they were forced to do any job that came their way, no matter how menial, in order to survive. This was especially true of those who settled in the Kalyan refugee camps, today the township of Ulhasnagar near Mumbai. The men hawked cheap goods on trains and in the city, and the women prepared and sold poppadums and pickles. I was told of one couple who apparently took to making soft drinks at home, which they then sealed in small plastic bags. The husband would balance the bags on his bicycle and hawk them around in the city. In three years, they managed to save enough money to invest in bottling machinery and build a small business. Some years and much cycling down the line, they were earning one lakh rupees a month.

Perhaps the stories that best reflect the themes of hard work and business acumen are those we might affectionately christen 'tales of soap and sugar'. They are the stuff of legend among the Sindhis in Mumbai, and in India more generally. While other wares make the occasional appearance, the usual suspects are soap and sugar. The plot might be summed up and stylized as follows:

> When we first came to Bombay, our livelihoods left
> behind in Sindh, we did everything we could to make
> a buck. So, sugar cost, say, 1 rupee a kilogram, and was
> sold in bags of 50 kilograms. We Sindhis hit on an idea.
> We would buy bags of sugar at retail price and sell on
> the streets at 99 paise a kilogram. What with our price
> being 1 paisa cheaper, our sugar sold well and we would
> move hundreds of bags—at a loss of 50 paise per bag.
> People wondered why we worked so hard only to lose

money. What they did not know was that we were selling
the empty bags at a rupee each, thus turning a profit of
50 paise for every bag of sugar.

Such stories may or may not be apocryphal. But
either way, they do tell us rather a lot about the early
ventures of Sindhi Partition refugees. It seems that
turnover was given precedence over profit margins.
Of course, turnover usually meant long hours and
self-exploitation, especially in the case of very small
businesses. Many Sindhis started out in ways—hawking,
for example—that required little if any initial capital and
were possible for people who had not much by way
of cash, other assets, or creditworthiness. It is worth
keeping in mind that not all Sindhis could draw on the
pedigree of networked Karachi merchants, Hyderabadi
Sindhworkis or Shikarpuri shroffs. Back in Sindh,
many Hindus had been local banias who earned a living
in small-time shopkeeping, trade or moneylending.
At Partition, they lost what immovable property they
may have had, as well as their businesses and debtors.
While some did manage to take with them cash and
portable objects of value, notably jewellery, this was
clearly not enough to finance the leap from local small-
scale business in Sindh to making a living in a city which
enjoyed a reputation as the '*urbs prima in Indis*' ('India's
foremost city'). If the gulf was to be bridged, it had
to be through hard work and enterprise. Hence, the soap
and the sugar.

Thus far in this book, I have looked at some of the
more dramatic journeys of Sindhis in Central Asia and
around the world. I shall now turn my attention to the

many thousands who graduated from soap and sugar to more profitable things in India itself. My focus will be Mumbai, and I shall proceed by taking up four of the more noteworthy examples of Sindhi enterprise.

Bankers and Moneylenders

Since Partition, Sindhis in India have done business in a range of fields, including export, investment, leasing, real estate and development, textiles, electronics, jewellery, hospitality, hardware, travel, car dealership and advertising. Of considerable interest are the bankers and moneylenders. As we have seen, historically this sector was predominantly the preserve of the Shikarpuris. In the late nineteenth century, and following the upheavals in Afghanistan in 1839–42, the Shikarpuri moneylenders seem to have shifted their trade to Russian Central Asia, among other places. This was to last until the period of the Russian Revolution. Especially following the fall of the khanate of Bukhara to the Red Army in 1920, the Sindhis moved their networks to south Asia.[2] The interwar period saw them active and thriving in various parts of the subcontinent, with at least fifty firms operating in and from Bombay. The number increased further after Partition, and at one point there were probably around 250 firms in Bombay and another 150 or so in other Indian urban commercial centres, notably Madras (present-day Chennai), Madurai, Trichinopoly (present-day Tiruchirappalli), Calcutta (present-day Kolkata), Hyderabad (in today's

Telangana) and Bangalore (present-day Bengaluru). While they had mixed operations back in Sindh, Shikarpuris in India after Partition were as a rule, not concerned with agricultural credit. It is for this reason that their business tended to be concentrated in the cities. While moneylending was an important facet of Sindhi settlement and business in India for decades, for many reasons, the number of moneylenders among them is today much reduced. Thus, my qualified use of the past tense.

Shikarpuri shroffs were bankers and financiers. Drawing on their creditworthiness, they acted as intermediaries between commercial banks or private investors and borrowers, typically merchants, real estate developers and small traders. As such, they were formally classified as 'indigenous bankers'. As defined in a 1931 official report, they were 'those individuals and firms who accept deposits or rely on bank credit for the conduct of their business and are close to or on the periphery of the organised money market and are professional dealers in short-term credit instruments for financing the production and distribution of goods and services'.[3] In their role as brokers between banks and borrowers, their key bureaucratic instrument was a promissory note or contract drawn up between the shroff and the borrower, on the strength of which the shroff dealt with the bank. There was a fixed credit period (ninety days, typically), and the size of loans varied according to the borrower's needs and creditworthiness. When a substantial loan was needed, it was not unheard of for a group of shroffs to spread risk by joining forces in a financing consortium, and any one shroff usually had access to and made use of a number of banks. Crucially, there were also brokers who acted as middlemen between the shroffs (themselves middlemen, given the involvement of banks) and the borrowers, which often helped to spread risk even more widely. Their various strategies for minimizing risk made sense, especially since shroffs were generally willing to provide unsecured loans. As one shroff put it, 'We used to give loans without much security, but keeping a very sharp eye on the person's business by way of eventually recovering the money'. It was, after all, this willingness that distinguished them from the commercial banks, and that kept them in business. It also helped that loan terms were negotiated and customized according to the particular needs and borrowing history of individual businesses. In India, then, Shikarpuris made up a tissue of finance which brought together investors and commercial banks and borrowers on the ground; the investors and borrowers could be, but were not necessarily, Sindhis. Within this tight-knit network, risk was dispersed and managed; informally, through mechanisms of social control, and in some cases formally, through legal structures. The financial worthiness of borrowers was perennially under the watchful eyes of tiers of brokers and their social circles: 'When a borrower defaulted, word spread like wildfire.'

There were two sets of relations of trust involved in these transactions: one between the commercial banks and the shroffs, and one that brought together the shroffs and their debtors. With respect to the first, the shroffs had over the years built their individual and collective creditworthiness with the banks through a combination of family reputations that were, in some cases, passed down the generations, and the practice of underwriting loans: that is, in case of default by the debtor, the shroff still honoured his part of the transaction with the bank. The general view is that default was rare—as one shroff put it to me, 'We Shikarpuris observed scrupulously our obligation not to default . . . we saw it as a social obligation that affected all of us, collectively, and we honoured all the contracts that were endorsed by the banks.' The fact that collective and individual 'honour' and reputation were interlinked cannot be overstated. This also means that there was a marked degree of in-group social control, since shoddy practices by unscrupulous individuals risked damaging one and all. The individual shroff was accountable to the banks, but also to his fellow shroffs. It was a matter of mutual benefit.

Equally finely balanced were the relationships between the shroffs and their debtors. Once again, reputations ran in families, even as they required periodic replenishment by individuals within those families. Understandably, Shikarpuri shroffs were cautious in this respect. Although circumstances did at times dictate otherwise, they preferred where possible to limit their business to debtors who were known to them. It was social control rather than some vague notion of ethnic solidarity that was at play. One's reputation was a key part of one's capital. As a shroff told me, 'At one point in Mumbai, up to 80 per cent of Shikarpuris were in the finance business. Most of us financed Sindhi trade. This is not because we paid attention to the caste (...)* of our debtors, but rather because we always tried to finance people we knew well and trusted.' Another Sindhi source of mine had a similar explanation: 'It's not that we especially identified with merchants who were Sindhis like us. But if a person was known to us and his reputation solid, we took risks. If not, we were cautious.'

Social control, then, was of the essence. It was in the shroffs' interest—and ultimately in the interest of the whole system, since sustained malpractice and default would destroy an important source of parallel finance—to see to it that high levels of social control existed, to supplement the institutional and other forms of sanction wielded by the commercial banks. One shroff who was in business for many years told me, 'News of default spread very quickly, by word of mouth. There would be a loss of trust in the person, he would lose his reputation for integrity. The trust on which everything was based would be undermined.' A debtor who failed to honour his commitments within the credit period became a 'marked man' who usually found it difficult, if not impossible, to secure further loans. This explains why Shikarpuri shroffs formed such a tight network in Mumbai: it was essential that information flowed quickly and freely, and that a shroff was able to assess the reliability of a would-be borrower based on his credit history within the network. 'The essential skill was to assess a potential borrower, not only financially, but also morally—is the person honest enough? Especially when a person came to us without any references, it was about reading body language and so on. It's an art'. The centrality of trust and image rubbed off on Shikarpuris as a whole, and it is they among the Sindhis who were known for certain attributes: 'We Shikarpuris value reputation a lot more. For us, not to pay back or not to keep your word is devastating. Shikarpuris are also less ostentatious, more sober.'

In view of this, it makes sense that many Shikarpuri finance businesses in Mumbai were clustered in one neighbourhood, Kalbadevi, to the extent that it was not uncommon for a number of different businesses to share the same office block. More formally, most of the shroffs were members of the Shikarpuri Shroffs Association Limited (incorporated in Bombay on 11 September 1944), which in 2000 had over 350 businesses on its list. The Association concerned itself with observance of the rules of business by its members, the safeguarding of members' interests and their relations with authorities such as the Reserve Bank of India and Government of Maharashtra. It did not, as an Association, involve itself in litigations between individual members, which were usually settled through private legal action. The fact that many of the shroffs operating in Mumbai were registered with the Association shows the importance of regulatory structures in such a vulnerable business as theirs.

When I visited in 2001, the Association's headquarters
on Kalbadevi Road consisted of little more than a desk
and a filing cabinet, but I did note a constant stream
of people coming and going, arguing and discussing
the business lives of others—'sharing experiences',
as I was told.

In some situations, and especially if they happened
to have particularly solid finances, Shikarpuri shroffs
could act as moneylenders without recourse to banks.
In Mumbai, for example, shroffs were behind the
financing of a good number of Bollywood films.
Given the scale of money involved and the whims
of cinema audiences, this was risky business indeed,
but it was also one in which the potential dividends
were vast. To minimize risk, films were often
financed in instalments, depending on the success
of the producer in selling film rights to territories in
India. The financiers would also sometimes reserve
the right to withhold the final print until most of the
dues were cleared. Collectively, Shikarpuri shroffs
enjoyed substantial private capital: in 1969, the
aggregate capital of 319 firms was tentatively—and
probably conservatively—estimated at Rs 16.4 crore.[4]
Shroffs could also tap into the financial resources of
friends and relatives, who were encouraged to deposit
private capital with them at interest. The world of the
Shikarpuri shroffs was a complex web of commercial
relations, both formal and informal, that brought
together moneylending, banking, brokerage, trade,
industry and entertainment.

For the community, it was also a rollercoaster world of trying to adapt to shifting circumstances. In the course of the twentieth century, the shroffs had to deal with the nationalization of the banks in 1969, as a result of which, banks came under state pressure to eliminate middlemen; 'loan melas' were held to encourage people to borrow directly from banks, although, as one shroff told me, 'most of that money was never retrieved'. Earlier in 1935, Shikarpuri shroffs had been offered full integration into the formal system by the Reserve Bank of India, only for the deal to fall through when the shroffs refused to open their books for inspection. Shroff firms also faced competition from Non-Banking Finance Companies (NBFCs). This chequered history notwithstanding, the fact remains that for the Sindhi trade and retail business in Mumbai and elsewhere, the presence of and links with Shikarpuri shroffs were an invaluable part of their development.

This might seem odd, considering the strong presence of commercial banks in metropolitan settings and the relatively high rates of interest charged by the shroffs. There was, however, a rationale to what may be called a parallel system of finance. As in the case of other groups of indigenous bankers—the Nattukottai Chettiars, Marwari Kayas and Gujarati shroffs—the services of Shikarpuri shroffs offered certain advantages when compared with those of the commercial banks. This was especially so in the world of small business. Shroffs offered a prompt, flexible, personalized and, above all, informal service.

Because loans could be unsecured, any would-be collateral was often left available to the borrower to make productive use of. Even if the interest rates were relatively high, loans were tailor-made to meet the needs of individual borrowers. Finally, and perhaps most importantly, banks were unlikely to extend loans to newcomers who had no collateral or security. It was here that the shroffs thrived, as sources of short-term capital that enabled the setting up of new businesses. The upshot is that at any point in time, Sindhi businesses could rely on composite financing, depending on what they could place as security and the particular nature of the loan they required. Even if people tended to shift from the informal to the formal sector as their business grew and became more creditworthy, the option of Shikarpuri shroffs remained a useful one to some.

There were many reasons why the moneylending business of Shikarpuri shroffs eventually dwindled. Especially in the major cities, it had to contend with competition from banks, which were increasingly willing to deal directly with borrowers. Rates of interest for commercial lending tended to go down. Increasingly, shroffs found they had to rely on their own capital, as opposed to serving as brokers between banks and borrowers, and it also became increasingly difficult to recover loans. As for the funding of films, alternative financing by the underworld or global corporations made Shikarpuris all but redundant. The result of these and other shifts are that few Shikarpuris rely solely on moneylending for their income. They might retain it as a side-business, usually in conjunction with other, newer, lines. There is change, then, but also continuity, because historically, Shikarpuris often combined moneylending with trade, as discussed earlier in this book. This is how Ram, a Shikarpuri from a moneylending family I spoke to in 2020, described the fortunes of his family:

'My ancestors originally did business in Iran. When the Russian Revolution broke out, they looked elsewhere. My grandfather came to India in 1931 and set up shop in the south, in Trichinopoly. Most of the money used to come from wealthy private lenders in Shikarpur, and it was in turn, loaned out to local businesses at higher rates of interest. Part of the family was based in India, the rest back in Shikarpur, from where they organized the funding. At Partition, they lost pretty much everything at home. In 1959, my grandfather set up shop in Bombay, again lending money to local businesses. His debtors were not for the most part Sindhis, but rather local shopkeepers, people looking to open small factories, or those who needed money for their daughters' weddings. His business did well until the 1980s, when the banks started lending money more liberally and at better rates. That hurt our business immensely, even if there were occasions when the banks used to contact us to find out about the creditworthiness of this or that individual. In my case, I was not particularly attracted to the family business and the constant and growing problems with borrowers. So I studied as a chartered accountant and eventually set up my own business, which had nothing to do with moneylending.'

Made in USA

Ulhasnagar is part of the Mumbai Metropolitan Region. The town has a population of over half a million, of which around 400,000 are Sindhis—it has, in fact, the largest concentration of Sindhis anywhere in India. It was officially named and declared a township in 1949, and can be traced directly to the Partition exodus. A significant number of the 341,000 Hindu Sindhi 'displaced persons' (refugees) who moved to what was then Bombay State were offered housing of sorts in the sprawling army barracks (camps) in the Kalyan area. The majority of them hailed from modest trading and business backgrounds in Sindh: the wealthier merchants and other established elites, who had the means and connections to rent or buy property, tended to settle directly in Bombay. Quite apart from its living conditions being dire, the new location was far from ideal. Sindhis found themselves isolated in a semi-rural district, whose inhabitants spoke a language (Marathi) foreign to them, and where the opportunity to trade and do commerce was all but absent. Attempts by the Indian government to absorb the Sindhis into the public and industrial sectors did not do much to solve the problem. Initially, the refugees were vociferous in their reluctance to accept the Kalyan camp as their new home. (Their reasoning was that there were no commercial opportunities whatsoever in the area). However, as it became clear that the Indian government was in no mood to provide them with accommodation in Bombay, they realized that they had to find creative ways around the problem.

One solution was to commute to Bombay. Statistics for 1956 indicate that about 10,000 residents of Ulhasnagar commuted daily to Bombay.[5] The town, however, was over 50 km from downtown Bombay, and the journey was—and still is, for the considerable number that still commutes this route—a major discomfort. The grim joke was that you never quite knew what your wife looked like, as you never got to see her face in daylight. The other solution was to stay put, to think of Ulhasnagar as a sort of commercial satellite of Bombay, and to tap into the insatiable appetite of the metropolis for all manner of goods and services. The Indian government offered help to the displaced persons in the form of soft loans and training in industrial skills. A Vocational Training Centre was set up in Ulhasnagar in 1948 by the Government of Bombay with the aim of teaching the immigrants technical skills, from making beedis to bookbinding, and from tailoring to pickling. A good number of the Sindhis who attended these courses did eventually set up their own small businesses. The government effort at training was paralleled by an attempt to form cooperative societies for manufacturing—but this scheme failed to get off the ground, and the socialist experiment invariably gave way to individual and family enterprise. Government loans were not the only route to capital for the Sindhis of Ulhasnagar. Some of them managed to save money from hawking and small-scale retail, while others benefited from family and group corpocracy. This is how Girdhar Balani (pseudonym), in his seventies when I interviewed him in 2005, and a refugee from Sindh who settled in Ulhasnagar, described his journey of securing finance during his early attempts to set up business:

> At Partition, we left our homes hoping that we would eventually go back. Many of us lost everything and had to start a new life; we were lodged in camps, and any chances of starting afresh in business were slim because we had little to no capital. We sold small, cheap goods and tried to set aside some of the profit. Some of us got loans from the Shikarpuris. In my case, I got a technical education and then a job, and managed to save some money—a couple of thousand rupees over a few years, but I used it to convince the bank to lend me Rs 10,000 to start my business. It was not easy, because the banks were reluctant to give loans to people who had little or no security.

Given the circumstances, it is not surprising that false starts were the order of the day. Ulhasnagar was described by one scholar in 1951 as being 'like the mythical town where all the people tried to live by taking in each other's washing'[6]. While government loans went a long way in making it possible for the refugees to open small shops and stalls, many soon ran into cash flow problems and closed down.[7] Even so, the proverbial ability of Sindhis to bounce back meant that by the late 1950s, Ulhasnagar had taken shape as a significant enclave of small industries and wholesale businesses. A contemporary official report says it was 'astir with small shops and small-scale industries'[8], and people from the surrounding areas of Ambernath and Ordnance Estate had warmed up to it as a place where a range of goods could be had at good value.[9]

Ulhasnagar today is a sprawl of apartment blocks, shops, workshops and industries. There is a central bazaar which runs through several streets and includes the cloth bazaar, the furniture bazaar, and the 'Japani' bazaar (where a range of imported items are sold), among other marketplaces. Many of the shops bear Sindhi names, including the ubiquitous 'Jhulelal'. The town emblem is a busy composite of self-perceptions and representations, and includes an earthenware jug with a swastika symbol, a palla fish symbolizing the Indus and the cult of Jhulelal, a briefcase and an academic hat representing education, and factories, a test tube and a sewing machine signifying the various trades and industries pursued by the Sindhis. Minimalist it might not be, but the emblem is a proud statement of the fact that in a couple of decades the Sindhis managed to transform the place from a dilapidated army barracks into a thriving and busy industrial and commercial township. It is an important chapter in the story of Sindhi business, because it is an example of Sindhis going into the manufacturing industry, as opposed to staying in the commercial sector they were more usually active in. While by no means unique— Sindhis in Nigeria, for example, have been involved in manufacturing for decades—Ulhasnagar is significant nonetheless, certainly for its scale and place in the history of Indian business, more broadly speaking.

There are, in fact, thousands of Sindhi-run businesses in Ulhasnagar. Many are small-scale: a printing press in a tiny room, a small warehouse for the wholesale of garments, and so on. Others Sindhis here may do subcontracting work for larger manufacturing companies: making a particular flavour for a biscuit brand, for example, or panel hinges for steel cupboards. The range of goods and materials produced here is mind-boggling and includes textiles, plastics, rubber, chemicals and paints, enamelled wares and electrical cables, pickles and spices, lighting and chokes, furniture, kerosene stoves, packaging materials, food products such as biscuits and bread, and pens and stationery. The goods and services traded include transport, car parts, textiles and jewellery.

Enterprise in Ulhasnagar tends to be close-knit. There is a marked degree of networking among the industrialists and merchants in the Sindhi community. The size of the town and the fact that business connections are embedded in the Sindhi social fabric mean that people have intimate knowledge of who produces or sells what. Thus, a Sindhi businessman looking to source a particular product in Ulhasnagar might not know the supplier personally, but would probably know someone who does. This tight-knit structure is expressed formally through various organizations, the most prominent of which is the Ulhasnagar Manufacturers Association. In 2000, the Association had 508 members on its list, '99.5 per cent' of whom were, according to its president, Sindhis. Apart from the Association, there are guilds set up by some lines of manufacturing. All of this breeds intense competition, but also a mutually beneficial interdependence.

The reputation of Ulhasnagar as a hothouse of enterprise and commercial energy has a more colourful side too. Especially in Mumbai, the name immediately conjures up images of counterfeit brands and goods that turn out to be not quite what they seem. While the association lingers on, often half in jest or in the form of stereotypes, it has its roots in a time when India was relaxed about patent protection. Besides, in the post-Independence years up to the early 1990s, import restrictions and exorbitant import tariffs meant that '*phoren*' (foreign, mockingly) goods, often smuggled into the country by 'couriers', were highly desirable. The joke is that the stalls and bazaars of downtown Mumbai had not got the memo. They were, in fact, awash with goods proudly labelled 'Made in USA'—only, 'USA' stood for 'Ulhasnagar Sindhi Association'.

The decline of protectionism and the subsequent flooding of the Indian market with imported brands did not necessarily starve the mimics. On the contrary, the rising tide of brand prestige tends to float the fake boats very well indeed. (The more desirable and expensive the Rolexes produced in Switzerland, the more reason for fakers to invest in better lookalikes.) For a long time, the Sindhi businesses of Ulhasnagar were synonymous with the manufacture of fakes. While this may sound an unkind thing to write, it is a matter that the protagonists themselves are ambivalent about. On the one hand, they feel strongly that this stereotyping does not do justice to the thousands of Sindhis who worked hard, and against the odds, to establish enterprises that produced quality goods. On the other, they are pragmatic about it as testimony to Sindhi artfulness in the face of adversity. I was once invited to dinner at the home of a wealthy Sindhi industrialist who owned a couple of factories in Ulhasnagar. He kept us entertained with talk of the provenance of what was on the table: 'fake poppadums', 'fake chikki', 'fake whisky', and so on. While there was nothing fake about any of them, and certainly not about his hospitality, he evidently found the stereotyping of his community quite hilarious. Some of my Sindhi sources in the area also told me about an 'insurance scheme' which some Sindhis from Ulhasnagar had come up with to make some money on the side, even as they commuted by train. Passengers would board without buying a ticket; instead, they would pay a Sindhi fellow commuter—the 'insurer'—a few rupees. In the unlikely event of a visit by a ticket collector, the fine would be paid by the insurer. For the insurer, the prospect of profit lay in the sporadic nature of inspections. Again, this may well be apocryphal, and certainly not without a dollop of humour. The point is, however, that these little jokes and stories serve the purpose rather well. They brilliantly convey the sense of risk-taking, enterprise and business savvy that Ulhasnagar has come to represent.

Textiles Traders and Commission Agents

Walking north from the Kala Ghoda and Fort neighbourhoods of Mumbai, one leaves behind a clutch of Gothic Revival and Indo-Saracenic buildings set in wide streets and spacious maidans and enters what can, to the uninitiated, feel like a chaotic world of sounds, smells, and all manner of traffic. This is Kalbadevi, one of the prime historic commercial districts of the city and home to importers, wholesalers, bazaar-style retailers, moneylenders and a few large merchant houses. The Sindhi merchants of Kalbadevi tend to cluster along Kalbadevi Road and around the eponymous Hindu temple. Nondescript doorways lead onto narrow passages lined with row upon row of small textiles businesses, where traders sit buried among fabric samples, piles of papers and account books, and customers discuss prices, sipping hot chai. When I visited in 2003, two such markets were the Swadeshi and the Kakad, situated within a stone's throw of each another and occupied by Sindhis as well as Gujaratis. The ground floors were taken up by the textiles shops, and the upper ones by the offices of the merchants and commission agents.

The concentration of Sindhi textiles traders and merchants in Kalbadevi is yet another example of business development among the community since Partition. Before that, the markets were for the most part occupied by the trading communities consisting of mostly Marwaris, Gujaratis and Bohras, who constituted the backbone of commerce in Bombay. The relatively small Sindhi presence in Kalbadevi involved Sindhwork firms, whose offices there ran an important part of the trade in textiles and curios. The city was a hub in the Sindhwork network, and most of the larger firms especially had extensive operations there. In some cases—Kishinchand Chellaram's, for example—the firms still do business in Mumbai. It was, however, only with the arrival of Hindu refugees that Sindhis became a substantial presence in Kalbadevi— and in the city more broadly, for that matter.

For the newly arrived, competing with the established trading groups was not easy. It was a matter of perseverance and skill, and of negotiating and forging alliances in order to carve out a space for themselves. Kakad Market is a good example of this. It had originally been set up by a Marwari textiles merchant, who in time came to do business and to get to know a number of Sindhis. When he eventually sold the place, the buyers were, quite naturally, Sindhis; this explains their presence there today. It is, of course, not just in Kalbadevi that Sindhi textiles traders do business. They are dispersed throughout the city, and their presence is notable in places like Khar, Andheri and Bandra. More broadly, tens of thousands of Sindhis are in the textiles trade across India, usually concentrated in localized markets and bazaars.

In Mumbai, besides being in the retail trade, they are typically in wholesale trade too, or act as middlemen between manufacturers and retailers. A number of businesses are involved in the brokerage trade as commission agents. The idea is to facilitate transactions between suppliers and retailers looking to source goods. The latter are often from outside the city, which can mean that they would be unfamiliar with the range of prices and quality available there. The commission agent's role is to help them navigate their way around the markets and secure the best deals; sometimes, the role extends to helping them with matters like accommodation during their buying trips in the city. It is also common for agents to stake their own creditworthiness in order to secure goods on credit for the buyers. For these services, the agents take a cut on the value of the transaction.

Take Raj, a Sindhi who runs a textiles shop in a small provincial town in Maharashtra and regularly sources his stock from the Mumbai markets. When in Mumbai, Raj stays at lodgings run by his commission agent, with whom he has a business relationship that goes back many years. The lodgings consist of a large room in a block of offices in Kalbadevi, where the agent hosts his business visitors for the night in bedding spaces of six by three feet. Raj often uses this space during the day too, to work on his accounts and papers. His host provides three meals a day, plus the occasional cinema ticket or other perks—Raj, in other words, is treated like a house guest. This is only part of his happiness, since it is only through his agent's connections in the city that he can possibly navigate the maze of suppliers, prices and credit in Mumbai. For his part, the commission agent is something of an Hermes, in that he can speak both the language of the gods and that of humans. He has intimate knowledge of the offerings and the terms of the suppliers, and he is equally well-versed with the needs and prospects of Raj's, and his other clients', business.

As in the case of the Shikarpuri shroffs and the industrial manufacturers in Ulhasnagar, textiles traders in Mumbai form a tight-knit network underwritten by both formal and informal relations, the latter neatly illustrated by Raj's visits to the city. More formally, the Bombay Sindhi Cloth Merchants and Commission Agents Association was formed in 1960. As the name suggests, it covers the Mumbai area, and its statute establishes that only Sindhis may join. The main role of the Association is to help settle litigations between members, usually over credit default. When a dispute comes up, the Association, which has legally binding powers established by the Arbitration Rules of 1940 and 1996 (the Arbitration Act of 1940 was replaced by the Arbitration and Conciliation Act of 1996), brings together the two parties in order to establish the nature of the case, and appoints arbitrators. These are typically senior members of the Association and experienced textiles traders in their own right. Cases are heard at the Association's offices in Kalbadevi, and usually take three to four months to resolve. The two advantages of settling litigations within the Association are, first, the efficiency of proceedings and, second, the absence of stamp duty and other fees that going to court would involve. Typically, and for obvious reasons, the Association limits itself to disputes involving small-to-medium-sized transactions. The number of cases brought before the

Association is typically significant: among other things, this suggests that the volume of trade in the Sindhi textiles business is one to be reckoned with.

Construction and Real Estate Development

Another kind of post-Partition Sindhi business in Mumbai that deserves a special mention is construction and real estate development. Names such as the Hiranandani Group enjoy a high profile on the list of real estate entrepreneurs in the city. Hiranandani Gardens in the northern suburb of Powai is a vast and impressive gated complex that goes back to 1989 and was one of the first of its kind anywhere in the city. There are historical reasons why Sindhis are in the real estate business. They partly have to do with the development of cooperative housing in the city. Bombay during the early years of Independence had two ingredients for the successful growth of cooperative housing: a high demand from the thousands of refugees flocking to the city, and a set of enabling circumstances. It was a landmark period, and Sindhis in Mumbai today believe they were the pioneers of cooperative housing in the city.

One of the difficulties faced by the Sindhi Partition refugees was housing. That space was and is at a premium is endemic to Mumbai, a group of islands and a marshy mainland that rose to reclaimed prominence as one of India's great cities. Certainly, by the time the Sindhis got there en masse, housing had become an issue. Space aside, there was a general shortage of building materials, and the ubiquitous practice of key money meant that securing a place to rent required a cash payment upfront. Never ones to throw in the towel, Sindhis applied lateral thinking to come up with what is variously called the 'ownership basis' system. Many of today's Sindhi housing societies, in Mumbai and elsewhere, started life as ownership-basis blocks of apartments. We have a useful description in a 1962 government report:

> The system, in brief, is that an enterprising individual or group of individuals secures a piece of land and constructs a building thereon consisting of a number of self-contained flats. Each flat is then sold to an individual on payment of a lump sum amount ranging from Rs 10,000 to Rs 1,25,000 according to the situation, the floor area, the amenities provided, etc. Prices sometimes differ from flat to identical flat in the same building, apart from flats on different floors. The payment is taken either in advance or in instalments. An Agreement more or less in a standard form is executed between the purchaser and the builder on Rs 1.50 stamp.[10]

There was no getting around it: ownership basis or not, nothing could be built without the capital to buy land, labour and materials. Capital could be had if you had it, or if you borrowed it from a shroff. Failing that, all was not lost still. This is how Kishore Melwani (pseudonym), whose business life started in Mumbai and ended up in London many years later, explained it:

'In 1963, I started my own business with a princely capital of two rupees. One Friday evening I got in touch with a man who had been my friend back in Sindh. He had a 700-square-yard plot in Bombay which he was prepared to sell, provided I managed to find twelve people who were ready to buy flats on a pre-construction-deposit basis. I went to the Post Office and invested my capital in stamps and a receipt book. On the train back home, I met a fellow Sindhi and "sold" him a flat. He handed me a Rs 250 deposit there and then, for which I wrote him a receipt. A couple of days later I brought together a group of friends in Ulhasnagar, and in no time I had my list of twelve people who wanted a flat. Their first contribution was Rs 2,000 each, which made it possible for me to get the work started. Things went well, and within a few years I had grown a thriving business and built a further five blocks of flats on ownership basis, which eventually became cooperative societies. I became a rupee millionaire. At one point I had a Godrej cupboard stacked full of cash—the thought of the taxman told me it was wise to keep it separate from my bank balance. The one thing that had made it all possible was trust. I had no capital to speak of, as I told you, but I was known to fellow Sindhis as an honourable man who would keep his word. That's the only reason they trusted me with their money.'

Lack of capital was not the only reason why trust, nourished within Sindhi networks, was so essential. The quality of workmanship is a notoriously thorny issue in the Mumbai building trade, and there is no shortage of profiteering cowboy builders who resort to cheap and inferior labour and materials. Raj's clients would have expected him to do nothing of the sort. Another problem was, and is, delivering the goods on time, especially where pre-construction payments are involved. Stories circulate in Mumbai of people who lost good money, and of builders who took money from people even before they had the required permits, or whose work was a million miles off schedule. It is here that the Sindhis stepped in, drawing on the relationships with and social control of co-ethnics. In spite of the problems and litigations and failed promises (it would not do to romanticize anyone, and Sindhis are no exception) it was an experiment that by and large worked. What's more, it was often from such beginnings that some Sindhis went on to become major builders and real estate developers in the city.

These examples, while arbitrarily chosen and only vaguely generalizable, do tell us something about the development of Sindhi business in India. They portray people who, for the most part, weathered the social and economic rupture of Partition and managed to establish themselves in a number of market sectors and local contexts. This is not to say that they did not face great difficulties along the way. It must be remembered that in the immediate aftermath of Partition especially, Sindhis lived in India as refugees, with all the implications of that. There are many documented examples of local resistance to their presence, and especially to their perceived unorthodox and rapacious way with business.

One study we have takes us to Pimpri near Pune, where in the 1950s, about 8000 Sindhis lived in a refugee 'colony' with Maharashtrians for neighbours. Even by that time, many of the Sindhis had opened textiles shops and stalls, and others hawked goods on trains. Partly on account of their readiness to operate at lower profit margins and thus undercut the competition, they experienced considerable tension with the locals. They were often seen as devious: obtaining and defaulting on government loans, for example, or pretending to be unemployed to avoid paying rent on government-subsidized property. Their reputation was not helped by their alleged practices, such as the dilution of ghee, organized gambling and bootlegging. There was a widespread notion among the local Maharashtrians that 'the Sindhis are all rich and pretend to be poor . . . they were "dirty", "showy", "wealthy" or "luxury-loving".'[11]

A more recent example is that of the Indira, Bapu and Nehru bazaars in the walled city of Jaipur, where Sindhis set up a range of businesses, from small stalls to upmarket glitzy shops in the inner-city markets in the decades following Partition. On the one hand, they were figured and valued by the state as *purusharthi* (industrious), an attribution that helped embed them in the Nehruvian developmental agenda:

> The refugee, manifesting the churning caused by partition, emerged as a figure to be governed and managed within the limits of the new nation state, furthering its developmental imperative . . . Their 'purushartha' was embroiled in a history of wealth and

land in Sindh, credit economy of state-owned banks
and politics of urban transformation in postcolonial
India. A dominant trope of the governance of the refugee
during the Nehruvian period was its resignification
as a 'labouring body'.[12]

Away from state-sponsored tropes in the second
half of twentieth century, however, things were more
complicated. The figure of the newcomer-refugee,
while imagined as innovative and enterprising, did not
necessarily sit well with the narrative of an old-world,
princely city. Sindhis found themselves at the receiving
end of a discourse of resistance that lamented, among
other things, the excessive commercialization of a place
held up as 'heritage'. Industrious or not, Sindhis were
often thought to be not honest. Sindhi importers were
accused of flooding the Jaipur markets with imported
vegetable ghee, thus tainting an otherwise 'pure' city.
Thus, Sindhis were simultaneously included and
excluded from the urban space and its markets: 'While
the "walled city" absorbed them in the retail economy
and benefited from their entrepreneurial practices, the
recent resignification of the wall as "heritage" by the state
authorities has also made the position of Sindhi retailers
rather precarious in the new regime of valuation of
urban infrastructure.'[13]

These and other similar instances are what gave
rise to the derogatory stereotyping of Sindhis referred
to in the first paragraph of this book. I have said that
I do not intend to entertain them in the slightest.
Rather, the running theme of the Sindhi business

story, in India as elsewhere, is one of resilience, adaptation and constant innovation. It is the theme that underwrites figures as far removed from each other as the Shikarpuri moneylenders in Bukhara in the nineteenth century, Sindhworki textiles traders in Yokohama, and a small manufacturer of poppadums in the Ulhasnagar of the 1960s.

6. THE CULTURE OF BUSINESS

In Chapter 2, we saw how Seth Naomul's family expanded their business by travelling, by being innovative and enterprising in new places and markets, and by placing family members and Sindhi gumashtas in strategic locations. We also saw how generous they were with 'large numbers of Brahmins and fakirs'. What Seth Naomul described, was in fact, a culture of business, the building blocks of which are as functional today as they were 200 years ago. While no single part of this culture is unique to the Sindhis, the way they bring it all together deserves our attention. We must look, firstly, at the readiness of the Sindhis to move around, and as they do so, to explore and develop new markets and networks; and secondly, at how Sindhi businesses tap into the resource of ethnic community; and, thirdly, at some of the choices Sindhis make when investing and spending money.

Mobility, Exploration, Innovation

Dieter Haller is a German anthropologist who has studied the Sindhis in Gibraltar. One of the things that struck him was that his Sindhi sources constantly welcomed relatives from all over the world, even as they themselves travelled and were hosted widely for business meetings, weddings or other family events.[1] I remember being equally impressed when I met my first Sindhis in Malta. Simply put, Sindhis are networked, and networked far and wide. To some extent or the other, their business and life histories refuse to be contained in any one place. Further, and to borrow the language of transport geography, their networks are of the hub-and-spoke, as opposed to the point-to-point, type. What this means is that there are places that have historically served as hubs, where more mobilities are made than can locally be consumed. Certain names come up again and again in the study of Sindhi business. Over the years they have included London, Mumbai, Hong Kong, east Africa and Japan. As expected, they are or were places of major Sindhi settlement—but the argument goes beyond population figures.

Take London. Especially after Partition, it grew into one of the hubs of the Sindhi diaspora. Not that this should terribly surprise us, because London is what social scientists call a 'global city'. In a nutshell, this means a city that operates in a geography which is profoundly global, although we usually have to add to that its local, national and regional bearings.

A truly global city is one whose presence permeates all corners of the world, even as it relies on them for its sustenance. The primacy of London is rooted in its history as an imperial capital, but the city also emerged in the post-colonial era as one of the busiest venues of global capital and cultural and social production. What's more, London is special even by the standards of global cities. Together with Tokyo, New York, Hong Kong and maybe one or two other metropolises, it belongs in the club of first-tier global cities. Look up any line-up of cities (and there are many), and London will be in or near pole position. A world of business like that of the Sindhis cannot help but connect to London, and then to connect some more.

The three major waves in which it did so were through Sindhwork, the exodus of Sindhis from east Africa in the late 1960s and early 1970s, and the modest but steady flow of migrants who moved to what used to be the capital of an empire within which they belonged. Even before Partition, some Sindhwork firms used London to help organize their network of branches and offices around the world. As the city gained traction as a hub of global finance and services in the course of the twentieth century, this presence became stronger. The Sindhwork network in London appears to have been tight-knit, with a concentration of businesses in the Moorgate area and at Salisbury House in particular. Sindhis socialized regularly at a local pub in Moorgate, and there was much flow of information, deliberate or not. A Sindhi trader who spent years as an employee of a firm told me how he had once decided to test the waters at another firm while pretending to be on vacation leave. Unfortunately for him, his boss was a regular at the Moorgate circle and it did not take him too many pints to find out what was going on.

The presence of Sindhis in London was boosted in no small way in the late 1960s and early 1970s by an exodus from the east African nations. British east Africa had for a long time been a major site of settlement and business operations for Sindhworkis, who were generally but not exclusively involved in import and wholesale trade. Even after Partition, east Africa had continued to attract Sindhis from India—mostly as employees of the Sindhwork firms, although many of them eventually set up their own businesses. The landscape changed in 1962 and 1963, when Uganda and Kenya, respectively, gained independence from Britain. Although the Sindhis and other Indians living there became eligible for citizenship in these countries, many declined it. Then came the political process known as 'Africanization': in 1967, for example, the right of non-citizens to stay in Kenya for any length of time was severely limited. Deprived of their right to do business or indeed to reside in the country, non-citizen Indians suddenly found themselves dispossessed. Between September 1967 and March 1968, approximately 12,000 Indians left Kenya to settle in Britain. In Tanzania, government restrictions on commerce practically killed off private firms by 1970. In Uganda, Idi Amin came to power in 1971 and duly proceeded to single out south Asians as endogamous, socially segregated and economically non-integrated undesirables. Oppression followed oppression, and in 1972 all south Asians were expelled from the country. A total of 28,600 refugees moved to Britain between September and November of that year. By the late 1960s-early 1970s it was evident throughout most of east Africa that the era of free commerce (and in Uganda, of the right of residence) was over and that Indians, Sindhis included, had no future there. It was an outcome that robbed those national economies of the spirit of enterprise, and thousands of people of their homes. Their solution was to move elsewhere, and a significant chunk of the Sindhis living in London today are the direct result of that move.

In addition to the old Sindhworki presence and the migrants from east Africa London in the second half of the twentieth century was the choice destination for substantial numbers of Sindhi migrants. Some held qualifications from technical or other colleges in India, while others were just motivated types who followed the lure of job opportunities in a global city. It was not always an easy ride. Santosh is now the proud owner of a thriving electronics business, which he runs from a well-appointed office in north London: 'When I first arrived here, I worked nightshifts for six weeks in a dry-cleaning firm, savouring all the wondrous smells of piles of dirty washing. I then joined K. Chellaram, for whom I had worked for three years in India. Eventually, I started my own business with my brother-in-law.' Among the difficulties Sindhi migrants faced was racism. Ram, for example, moved to Britain from Kenya (where he held a good clerical job with the British Army) in the late 1960s: 'When I came to London, the racism was unbelievable. People made fun of my accent, even though I spoke excellent English. After years of service with the army in Kenya, I came here to be offered a job as a doorkeeper.' Dharam, a qualified engineer from east Africa who got a job with a British company run by a 'particularly enlightened Britisher', remembers how clients often would not hide their disappointment that the company had assigned them an Indian engineer. Racism and discrimination were among the reasons why many incoming migrants sought employment with Sindhwork firms. As one informant put it to me, 'At least they were Indian like us.' For their part, the Sindhworki bosses were only too keen to employ Sindhis: they were part of a known social network, but they were also easier to exploit ('English employees looked at the time and asked for their rights').

The outcome of these different currents of migration is that today there are a few thousand Sindhis in London. Most live in north and central London, and there is a physical and social faultline that divides 'central London' and 'suburban' Sindhis. The former tend to be older-money families whose background is Sindhwork, and whose business and social connections extend well beyond London, or indeed the UK. 'Suburban' Sindhis, on the other hand, are usually people of rather less grand means, whose families migrated from east Africa or India in the second half of the twentieth century. There is, of course, some blurring here: homes in some of the more affluent suburbs can be very expensive indeed, and there are also people whose modest beginnings in the 1960s and 1970s have turned into something else that makes central London living possible. That said, the distinction is alive and well among Sindhis themselves, who often talk about the different lifestyles of the two groups and about the aloofness of the central London Sindhis, who inhabit a world of their own. The experience of Lila, who comes from a multimillionaire Sindhworki family and lives in the smartest part of South Kensington, suggests there is some truth to this. She socializes mostly with Gujarati, Marwari, Punjabi and Sindhi women who live in central London, and holds that wealth has a lot to do with her choice of friends: six out of her eight best friends, including three Sindhis, live on Avenue Road near Regent's Park, a stretch sometimes known as 'millionaires' row'. One notable characteristic of Sindhis in London today is that a good number of the younger people are moving into services (middle-managerial and consultancy jobs, for the most part), among other fields. Partly, the reason is that Sindhi families tend to give a lot of importance to education and paper qualifications, and are usually only too happy to fork out for post-graduate degrees, notably in business studies and management at well-regarded universities. There is no contradiction between tertiary education of this sort and business; on the contrary, the ability to fund an expensive education is seen as a prime indicator of family business success.

With respect to business itself, Sindhis who lost their businesses in east Africa or their jobs with Sindhwork firms there took up some form of (generally low-paid) employment upon moving to Britain, only to eventually set themselves up as self-employed. The majority of the Sindhis in London are in the import, export, wholesale and retail of consumer items, but there are Sindhi businesses in lines as diverse as financial services, real estate, engineering consultancy, restaurants and hotels, manufacture and information technology. A substantial number of Sindhis in London are in the electronics line, as evidenced by their presence on Tottenham Court Road, a hub of electronics wholesale and retail. In this context, it is telling how profoundly the routes of Sindhi business are tied up with shifting global conceptions of quality. In the early days of Sindhi operations in London (mainly from the 1930s to the 1960s) Sindhwork firms often sourced products from Britain for their wholesale and retail businesses in Africa and elsewhere; at the time, British manufacture was a byword for quality in the minds of many, while Japanese-made goods were seen as second-rate. As a trader who imported from Japan to east Africa told me, 'We used to joke that that stuff lasted a week and then died on you.' However, as the image of Japan-made electronics changed to one of dependable technology and affordability, established Sindhi business routes were simply reversed to milk the new global market trend. The Sindhis' interconnectedness shows up in other similar instances. According to my Sindhi sources, the 'hot line' in the 1970s was the import of watches and cheap electronics from Hong Kong, Taiwan and Korea; these countries specialized in such manufactures, and again Sindhis were well-equipped in terms of business connections to exploit the change. A significant number of Sindhi businesses in London tap into their connections with India and elsewhere to cater for the 'ethnic niche' market—that is, the large numbers of people of south Asian origin settled in the city who form a consumer base for items like Indian food and saris.

Another, perhaps more telling type of Sindhi business in London is that of the confirming houses, which among Sindhis were in their heyday during the 1970s and 1980s. The principle of the confirming house was summed up to me by a Sindhi who made millions in the business and now lives in a penthouse overlooking Regent's Park: 'A Sindhi importer in west Africa wants to import from Sindhi suppliers in the Far East, but he has no money. The suppliers do not know him, so credit is out of the question. So, the Sindhi confirming house steps in as a broker.' It was often the case that direct credit between the suppliers and the Sindhis based in Africa was hard to negotiate. Besides, many small traders based in Africa did not have the level of creditworthiness to go directly to the international banks. (With particular reference to Nigeria, there was the additional problem that Nigerian banks were reluctant to open letters of credit on behalf of exporters in the Far East.) Enterprising Sindhis in London saw their chance and set up confirming houses that specialized in this kind of high-risk brokerage. The confirming house in London would produce a letter of credit in favour of the supplier. As soon as the goods were shipped, the supplier would get paid by the confirming house, which in turn, extended a credit period to the importer in Africa.

The Sindhi confirming houses themselves were mostly financed by British and other banks that were based or had branches in London, although some of them also made use of their own private finances. They charged confirmation commissions of 3 per cent to 6 per cent, depending on the liability of the transaction and the stability of the country in question. As one confirming agent told me, 'Ten per cent would hardly have convinced me where Liberia was involved, while 3 to 4 per cent would be fair for a deal involving the US.' Apparently, some countries imposed charges on money remittances, which further inflated the commission charges. The credit period was equally variable, but was generally in the region of 90 days to 120 days from the day of shipment. In addition to these charges, the importer would have to pay the commission house the interest charged by the bank, plus any other expenses.

There were two types of confirming businesses. The first were known as 'house to house' and were owned by the firm itself, typically a large and established Sindhwork operation. Many of the big firms, with branches in several countries and generally involved in import-export but also sometimes in manufacture, had offices in London, which, because of its infrastructure as a global city (excellent communications, banks and so on), proved a fine location to coordinate business, and especially finance from. Apart from financing trade, these 'house to house' confirming houses acted as foils to siphon money out of Africa into the UK; the 'profit' made by the London company would ultimately be coming from the African branch owned by the same people. It was a creative way to spread assets, and one that was particularly important to firms operating in the fickle political and economic climate of west Africa. The second type were the so-called 'third party' or 'customer finance' confirming houses, which were separately owned and worked along the model explained earlier. Some Sindhi confirming houses in London had Gujarati and other clients based in west Africa, but the bulk of the trade took place between Sindhis. This did not necessarily extend to the suppliers, with whom relations of trust did not matter very much, given that they were getting paid by the banks. Because they were ready to extend credit to Sindhis based on trust, confirming houses served as excellent stepping stones for business start-ups that would otherwise never have managed to obtain credit from banks, let alone Far Eastern suppliers. As one confirming agent told me, 'In a way it was easier to start a business without initial capital, thanks to confirming houses.'

Confirming houses were thus a means by which Sindhi enterprise could take root, and they were often also the source of lucrative takings for the risk-takers who ran them. This was the case until well into the 1990s, when the business went into decline. The many reasons need not detain us here, but they included a swathe of defaults and growing mistrust, which pushed people to be more cautious. There were also unscrupulous brokers who took to creative accounting in order to inflate their commission charges.

London then, was, and is a hub of Sindhi business, but what about the spokes? How did Sindhis navigate the various markets they encountered and create new ones? I shall limit myself to two examples, chosen because they involve two places that are the very opposite of a global city. As it happens, both take us to islands that are considerably less prominent than the UK. The first is in the Caribbean, where Kishore, a Sindhi businessman, has lived and worked for the best part of four decades. Saint Martin (Saint-Martin/Sint Maarten) is an 87 km^2 island in the Lesser Antilles, two-thirds of which is a French overseas collectivity and the rest, part of the Kingdom of the Netherlands. When Kishore got there, quite by chance, there were thirty-four Sindhis living on the island. All were in the business of tourism and had formed an Indian Merchants Association a few years earlier. Kishore has seen the Caribbean tourism business grow exponentially, and with it, a big rise in the number of Sindhis looking for business opportunities in Saint Martin. Many of them moved to the island from Bombay, Pune, Madras and other places in India, as word spread that the tourism trade was booming. Today, there are about one thousand Sindhis in business in Saint Martin, out of a population of around 77,000. True to the local economy, they are mostly in tourism-related retail, but some are also in general imports. A few have ventured into the hotel business. Most of the Sindhis here live on the Dutch side of the island, where the laws and regulations are thought to make for more profitable business. Like many Saint Martiner Sindhis, Kishore is fluent in a number of locally spoken languages. He visits London at least once a year, for business and to visit family.

THE SINDHIS

The second example takes us to Port Blair, the only urban settlement of any significance in the Andamans, an archipelago and union territory of India situated about 150 km north of Indonesia in the Bay of Bengal/Andaman Sea. During the second half of the twentieth century, Port Blair developed into the residential and business centre of the islands. The busiest part of town is Aberdeen Bazaar, which is also where the Moorjanis (pseudonym) run their business. It started with Chandru, who was born in Karachi to a family of Hindu Sindhis that traded in ghee and other foods. At Partition, the family left Sindh, and after a short stint in Gujarat, settled in Bombay in 1948, where they set up a small business distributing and wholesaling pens and stationery (buying in Bombay and selling in Goa, for the most part). For over two decades, the family lived in the city in a Sindhi housing cooperative society. In 1972, however, Chandru went on a trip to the Andamans as a tourist. Snorkelling did not quite cut it, but the thought occurred to Chandru that this would be a good place to do business. Three months later he was on his way back to Port Blair, this time with a small stock of pens in his luggage. His hunch was right, and from 1972 to 1978, Chandru made frequent trips to the islands, where he sold pens sourced in Bombay. The journey from Madras took up to five days, and in Port Blair he took advantage of the hospitality of a Sikh gurdwara. Already at the time, there were flights to the Andamans, and hotels. But then his profit margins were slim, and cost-cutting measures helped preserve them.

In 1978, Chandru did what Sindhis do best. The decision to open a shop and settle in the Andamans was taken partly to cut risk. He had been selling wholesale, on credit, to local retailers, and the life of an absentee creditor can be tricky. Besides, his business back in Bombay had been dealt a blow by a dishonest partner. Chandru's son, Alex, joined his father in Port Blair in 1980, followed by Chandru's wife Sita soon after. Life in Port Blair was 'boring, with nothing much to do except work'. Chandru and Alex visited Bombay frequently to source pens and to coordinate things with Ram, Chandru's other son, who was posted in Bombay. The Moorjanis like to joke that they are now the Andaman 'king of pens'. Aside from importing, they also manufacture their own brand of pens, subcontracted through small businesses in Mumbai and Kolkata. They have also done something else that Sindhis do well—they have diversified. They import textiles and consumer goods from Mumbai, where Ram now runs a trading office in Kalbadevi district. The Moorjanis consider themselves well settled in the Andamans, where Alex is an active Lion and regularly patronizes social events held by the local business community.

For Sindhis, mobility, exploration and innovation go together, being often the route to business success, which is very much a matter of knowing where and when to buy and sell. Besides, their readiness to move has the advantage of cutting down on middlemen. As a young Sindhi bhaiband put it to me, 'Lack of family unity is the price we pay for being wealthy. Making money has a lot to do with spreading out members of the same family. The key Sindhi families, those leading the way in business, are all dispersed and living in several countries. Why else would one live in a dump like Nigeria, rather than live in a decent, settled country like the UK and pay taxes? Sindhis have tended to flock to corrupt, dumpy places—but no Sindhi believes that west Africa is there to stay.' So ingrained is this readiness to move that many Sindhi success stories come from politically unstable countries such as Liberia and Sierra Leone. In such places, the high risk of losing everything overnight minimizes competition, and maximizes dividends, for those who are prepared to take the risk. So much so, that some Sindhis refer to the notoriously corrupt Mobutu era (1965–1997) in the Democratic Republic of the Congo and Zaire as a 'golden age', during which 'there was a lot of prosperity as long as one did not interfere in politics—which we didn't'.

Classically, Sindhworkis were wont to go 'on tour' and scout for business opportunities. This was especially true in the days of sea travel, when they would explore the various stopover harbours and ports, but it certainly survived well into more recent times. Pishu, a bhaiband, described to me a 'tour' he had undertaken for the Sindhwork company with whom he was employed in the 1960s, and an opportunity he had come across: 'I went on tour on behalf of the firm. I visited African countries like Mauritius, Portuguese East Africa, Rhodesia, Northern Rhodesia . . . I took with me sixteen bags of samples plus the paperwork for any orders. Meanwhile, my bosses called me to Hong Kong and I went back via Bombay, Calcutta and Singapore. In Singapore I chanced across a Chinese company that manufactured a brand of shirt and made big money, and I suggested to my bosses that they look into it.' In this particular case, his bosses were not interested in shirts. But Pishu, who also had relatives in Singapore, was. He moved there and gave the shirt business a try under his own steam, but without much success, it must be said.

In addition to 'touring' for specifically business purposes, the constant rounds of family visiting, which so impressed Dieter Haller, often ended up doubling as business ventures, as information and sometimes samples of goods were picked up along the way. While having tea with a Sindhi family in London, I was told that they had once been to Malta to visit some people there in relation to the Sindhi-run Holy Mission of Guru Nanak: 'We went to the other small island, Gozo. There we saw the knitwear they made and brought over a suitcase full of jerseys to try and sell in the UK. It was hard to sell them, though, and we left it at that.' A similar explorative venture was described to me by Prem, who now runs a successful import-export business based in north London: 'Before I left Hong Kong, I bought a large quantity of Levi's jeans and air-freighted them. I knew they fetched good prices in Indonesia—I had been there you see, visiting my in-laws. They were seconds, rejected for the US market, and I bought them at half price from a Gujarati trader. I managed to turn a good profit on this sizeable consignment.'

A Business Community

It is a platitude one often hears—that the range of business opportunities available in the world is infinite and that it is quite impossible for any single trader, no matter how savvy and how diasporic his community, to be familiar with more than a handful. But if that trader happens to be part of a widespread business community within which information flows and transactions take place, his chances are greatly improved at pursuing a larger number of businesses.

A great many Sindhis do business with each other. The hub-and-spoke network I described earlier is not just about connections, but also about the information, goods, services and credit that flow along them. This helps Sindhis source the best-priced goods and to resell where there is the highest profit to be made. The Multani Trading Corporation (pseudonym) in Japan, for example, exports globally from Japan to wholesale and retail businesses in Hong Kong, Malaysia, Singapore, India, the UK, the US and the Canary Islands. About 60 per cent of its clients are Sindhi, most of whom are family or friends of family. Gilbert, who now runs an old Sindhwork family business in Malta, told me that if the country were to become a duty-free port, Sindhis would have a field day, what with the large numbers of relatives they had who were in business around the world.

Even so, it would be a mistake to imagine all Sindhis as one big happy family. As one trader put it, 'We Sindhis do not trust each other—we only do business with each other because we have to.' The truth is, they do not really have to—but where else would an aspiring business find the kind of connections that come with being part of a large and well-interconnected community? That these connections come with risks and tensions should be obvious, and best illustrated by a joke told to me by a Sindhi in London:

Two cousins lived on the same street. One night, there was light at the window of one of the cousins, Prakash, who paced the room nervously, unable to sleep. His wife asked him what the matter was, and he replied that his sixty-day credit limit with his cousin Mukesh, who lived opposite, was due the following day. He did not have the money to pay up. Calmly, his wife told him, 'Why worry? He's your cousin. Phone him now and ask him to extend the credit limit for a few days until you sell the goods.' It took a lot of convincing, but eventually Prakash saw sense and phoned Mukesh, who immediately and enthusiastically agreed to extend the credit. The weight off his shoulders, Prakash turned off the lights and went to bed. Fifteen minutes later the lights came on at the window across the street. There, pacing the room, was Mukesh.

Jokes aside, the network of family, community and business connections in the community helps us understand one of the key characteristics of Sindhi business. Sindhis tend to 'come back with a bounce' when things go wrong. Simply put, they have the infrastructure to be able to do so. Take the example of Sindhis in Tangier. From 1923 to 1956, the political status of Tangier was that of an international city governed by a commission composed of representatives of various countries. It was also variously a duty-free zone, and many Sindhis settled there in order to be able to re-export goods imported from the Far East to Europe; these goods were imported via Sindhis living in Hong Kong, then a major producer of consumer electronics. In 1956, however, the local commercial landscape changed. Tangier's integration with the independent Kingdom of Morocco meant that Tangier was no longer a duty-free haven, and Sindhi traders suddenly found it difficult to continue to operate. Most of them left the place, but they continued to draw upon their links and established credit lines with Sindhi exporters in Hong Kong in order to set up import businesses elsewhere. All of this lends credence to the Sindhis' saying of themselves that they 'change lines as easily as they change their clothes', and that they are able to do this because of Sindhi family and friends, who, each time are ready to provide them with credit and help them start, or restart, businesses.

A Word about Investment and Consumption

Throughout this book, I have argued that—and hopefully shown how—the culture of mobility is the cornerstone of Sindhi business. Invariably, that culture also translates into the ways Sindhis spend and invest their money. People on the move are often associated with remittances back home. Except in the case of Sindhis, the certainties of home were robbed by Partition. Among Sindhis, one rarely, if ever comes across the idea of eventual return to the homeland. Especially to the younger generations, Sindh is a socially remembered past which, while definitional, will never come back. Further, the numerous 'small partitions' brought about by political changes in east Africa and elsewhere render even less straightforward any notion of a timeless home. This probably explains why Sindhis, and especially those living outside of India, tend to keep a low profile and not involve themselves in politics. Sindhis have been in Malta for almost 150 years, for example, but the gut feeling that things could change anytime is not entirely absent, especially among the older generation. 'We're alright now, but what if a Maltese missionary was killed in India?', one businessman who has owned shops on the island his entire life told me. These fears are much stronger among Sindhis in some of the African nations, where the threat of political fireworks is never too distant. They are weaker among Sindhis in the UK, Canada, the US and other countries that generally enjoy a reputation for stability. Circumstances can also ebb and flow: the handover of Hong Kong to China, for instance, created a widespread, if fairly temporary feeling of uncertainty among the Sindhis living there.

There are two ways in which these fears can be allayed. The first is to spread assets, and by inference, risk. As one trader in London told me, 'Sindhis have a theory which has kept them going: never to keep all eggs in one basket. One gets used to this idea of having assets and interests in various places.' A business with branches in multiple countries is the safest bet of all, since this preserves at least some income should anything go wrong in any one particular place. The dividends of business, too, can be spread, and Sindhis are known to invest in real estate in Mumbai, London and elsewhere. A considerable number of Sindhis from west Africa own apartments in London, for example. They may actually reside there for at least a few weeks a year, or the properties may be used to host family members or young Sindhis studying in London. Nor is it just about risk. Owning property in one or more prestigious places makes for a cosmopolitan lifestyle, itself the twin of a mobile business culture. Wealthier Sindhis will often find themselves working in Nigeria, socializing in London and visiting Mumbai in December.

Spreading business assets and owning multiple properties allows for mobile lives. There are other such forms of investment, of which perhaps the most portable is jewellery, and especially diamonds. What follows comes with a health warning, because Sindhis have often been caricatured—in Bollywood films, for example—as flashy arrivistes. Perhaps it is more empirically accurate to head to a Sindhi wedding in Hyderabad in 1941, as described by a British guest:

> They ate everything with their fingers though we were given forks and it was an amazing sight to see dainty fingers laden with jewels—two of our host's single diamond rings were half an inch across—dipping into the greasy curry. Silver bowls were brought . . . Four bands

were playing all the time, one in complete Highland
uniform . . . The bride, by the way, was wearing the
most lovely silver and chiffon sari, the edges deeply
embroidered in pearls and diamenté . . . I was glad I did
'over dress' a little, as everyone's saris were so gorgeous.[2]

Again, there is nothing endemically Sindhi about
any of this. The anthropologist Helen Ward, who did
fieldwork in India, described gold and jewellery as a
'bank belonging to women'[3] and argued that 'much of
the value of gold in the Indian context derives from the
fact that it is commonly understood as a value which
is universal'.[4] Surely then, if the value of gold and
diamonds transcends locality, this makes them even
more attractive to people who prefer their wealth to
be invested in transportable ways. Gold and diamonds
are not just banks: they are international currency
that allow one to make withdrawals of cash or obtain
credit practically anywhere in the world. A bhaiband
now living in London expressed to me his love of
diamonds, and showed me an impressive looking stone
set in a ring. He told me that diamonds were a must
among Sindhis, and especially among the wealthier
bhaibands. He recalled that on his business trips from
Hyderabad to South Africa, his father used to smuggle
back to Sindh, diamonds concealed in a flashlight,
and that some Sindhis used to smuggle diamonds
back to Hyderabad in tins. Having said that, some
Sindhis who are well-versed in matters of international
finance argue that diamonds are just one, and not
necessarily always the best, form of investment. One
bhaiband who runs a business in the Democratic

Republic of the Congo told me, 'Unlike other people, I don't believe in investing my money in jewellery— rather, I go for bank savings. The world diamond market is controlled by one company, De Beers, and they could cut the value of diamonds at the drop of a hat.'

Finally, there is added value to this kind of investment. Because they are worn at weddings, kitty parties and family occasions at which Sindhi men and women from around the world meet, diamonds serve as a means to circulate the image of prestige and wealth of the family. By virtue of being worn on the body, they are conspicuous and mobile, and thus an ideal way to display wealth. The same goes for watches (preferably Rolex in precious metals), silk saris and designer handbags—all of which are very popular with well-to-do Sindhis around the world. It is for this reason that Sindhis are widely regarded as ostentatious. Caricature or no caricature, it never ceased to surprise me just how often Sindhis themselves bring the matter up. I should best leave the last word to a woman from a Sindhworki family: 'I was brought up in Jakarta in Indonesia. There, we Sindhis are very different from the Gujaratis and the Chinese in that we are big spenders—Sindhis are very showy people and spend money even if they don't have much. We often seem much wealthier than we actually are, you see.'

7. BIOGRAPHIES OF UNKNOWN SINDHIS

This final chapter, and certainly its title, comes with apologies to the late Nirad C. Chaudhuri.[1] It consists of ten biographical snippets, recounted here exactly as they were told to me. None are of high-profile Sindhis or their businesses, nor are any of the protagonists particularly known outside their circle of family, friends and business associates. They are, in this sense alone, unremarkable Sindhis. Read together, however, they do two things. They help us understand Sindhi business as it is actually lived, with all its ups and downs, and they also show how the many strands discussed in this book—Sindhwork, moneylending, business diversification, the events and costs of Partition, mobility, risk-taking—are interwoven in the individual life histories. Thus, the Chaudhuri connection. I use pseudonyms throughout, but have otherwise not changed the content in any way.

Sham Daswani

The story of Sham Daswani shows how family business legacies can function, at times in episodic ways that see individual entrepreneurs tap into family and group resources at strategic points in their working lives. Sham comes from a bhaiband family. On his father's side, his grandfather, and later his uncles, were in business in Japan, where they established themselves as Sindhworkis in the textiles trade before Partition. They later shifted to electronics, mainly the export of Japanese branded consumer electronics. Somewhat exceptionally, Sham's father was not in business with his father and brothers. In 1959, he moved to London from India 'with not a penny in his pocket', and worked for a few years at Ford in Dagenham. He then started buying and selling rugs, eventually at the Whitechapel and Petticoat Lane markets, where he had a stall from 1968. At one point, he started importing textiles sourced through his brothers in Japan and selling them in London, particularly to the Bangladeshis who were settled in the city. Sham has vivid, if not particularly fond, childhood memories of days spent with his father and brothers at the Whitechapel and Petticoat Lane markets. He remembers it was 'bloody hard work'—nothing new there, because his uncles in Japan routinely overworked themselves, ('they're crazy, they work till ten or eleven at night, every single day'). In due course, one of Sham's brothers opened a children's clothing shop in Petticoat Lane. The brothers worked together and trade was brisk, especially when they started importing clothes directly from Singapore through a Sindhi friend who was in business there. The Singapore connection was so good that they set up their own export office there and employed a local (non-Sindhi, that is) to run it. In 1996, Sham left the family business to set up his own women's clothing shop, this time importing from a number of sources in Singapore and elsewhere.

Mohan Raheja

Mohan and his son run a small business from an industrial estate in Andheri, Mumbai. Mohan was born in Karachi in 1935. Originally, the Raheja family were from Daraza in Khairpur District. Daraza was a small village. It was the burial place of the Sufi poet Sachal Sarmast (1739–1827) and a pilgrimage destination of note. Raheja is a typical Shikarpuri surname, and the family were small-time moneylenders who did business with traders in Karachi. In 1948, they had to leave Sindh. It was all very sudden and they lost most of their property and equally disastrously, the numerous debts they were owed as part of their business. Their first port of call in India was Bombay, but it was not easy to find accommodation there. So they moved to Delhi, then to Orissa, and on to Nasik, where they tried to set up in the textiles trade. Stiff competition from the local traders made it impossible for them to gain a foothold, however, and they moved from line to line without much success. Mohan told me that their experience was fairly typical, in that, generally it took the dispossessed Sindhis a difficult couple of decades to pick up the pieces of their shattered lives. This was particularly true of people from modest business backgrounds back in Sindh, who did not have good connections in India. Mohan's chance came when a Sindhi friend of his, who lived in Bombay, offered to help him open a small shop in the city, selling watches. The stock came on generous credit terms, and Mohan did his bit by selling at a relatively low margin of 10 per cent to 15 per cent. It was not all plain sailing: on one occasion, for example, the shop was burgled and all the stock was lost. But Mohan worked hard, and eventually employed a trained man to also offer watch repair. Watch-straps followed. Mohan would buy the materials and pass them on to a local (a Maharashtrian) who made the straps, which were then sold in the shop. Still, business was relatively slow, and Mohan took the gamble of wholesaling straps to other retailers. What gave him the much-needed edge was that he did so on a sale-or-return basis. It was a gamble that worked, especially since many retailers were otherwise not prepared to even consider stocking straps 'made by an unknown manufacturer'. Mohan's is now a thriving, if small watch-strap wholesale business, which is run mostly by his son, Arjun. The goods are not manufactured in-house but rather through subcontractors.

Laju Ramchand

Laju was not born into a business family: in Sindh, his father worked in the civil services. Laju himself was born in Bombay after Partition and went to school at Jai Hind College, a school established in the city by a group of Sindhis who had been teachers at D.J. Sind College in Karachi. As a teenager, and like many Partition refugees, he dreamt of studying and living in Britain. His chance came when his sister married a Sindhi who worked there. Laju made the journey for the wedding, and stayed on. He enrolled in a diploma course in industrial accounts, and to keep body and soul together, kept the books for a Sindhi importer in London who was his second cousin on his mother's side. For some reason, he returned to India after three years, but found that job opportunities and salaries were poor. So back to London he went, and this time his second cousin and former employer supplied him with some small goods (brassware, carvings, transistor radios, and so on) on easy credit to help him start his own business. So generous were the terms, he even had permission to get goods on credit from other sources, using the good name of his cousin's company as security. Laju had worked diligently during his time as an accountant, and he never once defaulted on his new responsibilities, but he does not doubt that setting up on his own would have been impossible without the help he got at this crucial stage. He was also greatly encouraged by his wife, who came from a bhaiband family and whose relatives ran small textiles businesses in Saigon and Japan. Her help was not limited to just encouragement, and they would work together at their small shop in the tourist run of Camden until eleven every night. In the 1980s, they diversified into the import and wholesale of consumer electronics, and did a brisk trade, especially in watches and calculators. When I interviewed Laju in 2005, he ran an electronics business on Regent Street, London.

Ram Nandwani

Ram Nandwani comes from a family of Hyderabadi bhaiband origin. Part of the family lived in their 'main house' in Hyderabad itself, and the rest in Hala New, about 50 km north of the city. In Sindh, their trade was in local textiles, mainly cotton. They would extend credit to (Muslim, for the most part) manufacturers, who would use it to buy cotton yarn. The Nandwanis would then trade the finished textile throughout Sindh, usually through Hindu middlemen. In this way, they combined trade with moneylending. There was a Sindhwork venture, too: in 1940, Ram's uncle took up employment with a Sindhi firm in Tripoli, except that war got in the way and he had to pack his bags and return to Hala. In 1947, the family left Sindh for Gwalior, where a cousin worked as a veterinarian in the cavalry section of the maharaja's court. The trip was not without its troubles: on the train from Hala to Karachi, a number of their suitcases were stolen.

Once they settled in Gwalior, the extended family pooled their resources and set up a joint business in 1948 as textiles wholesalers. It was not a good move. Ram reckons there were simply too many partners for the business to run smoothly, and there was also increasing direct competition from other Sindhis (most of whom had moved from Sukkur) in the Gwalior textiles trade. It did not help that the brokers hired by the Nandwanis were themselves from Sukkur and tended to favour the people from their own region of origin. In the event, the family business collapsed in 1954. Largely penniless, Ram ended up job-hunting in Lucknow, where he was put up by his sister who had married a Sindhi there. For seven years, Ram worked as a clerk with the Reserve Bank of India. He married a bhaiband woman in 1961, and the following year the couple moved to London, where his wife's brother ran a small business. In London, he soon got a job with K. Chellaram, which at the time was importing goods from Japan, among other things. Three years later, Ram joined his brother-in-law's business as a market seller on a commission basis. Things did not go as planned, and he went back to K. Chellaram, this time to work in the exports section. Some months later, it was his turn to be exported. A family friend, a Sindhi who ran a thriving business in London with his brother-in-law, was looking for someone trustworthy to employ. Ram was the obvious choice, at least until family tensions got in the way and he grew increasingly uneasy in this job. It so happened that one of the (Sindhi) companies that supplied the business he worked for got wind of this and offered him a job. For two years, Ram worked in the accounts section of that company, whose main line was import of electronics and other goods from Hong Kong, mostly through Sindhi suppliers there. (The company eventually went on to become a major concern, and its owners, at one point worth hundreds of millions of pounds, a fixture on the *Sunday Times* rich list.) Ram enjoyed a good salary and commission, and in due course was entrusted with managing an electronics wholesale branch in East London. When the main company sold the branch, it was Ram who was the successful bidder. He was eventually joined by his younger brother, who moved from India, and they run the company together with their sons. At one point, his brother was hived off to Hong Kong to supply goods directly to London, thus cutting down on middlemen.

Arun Moolchandani

Arun Moolchandani was born in Hong Kong in 1960. At the time, his father Suresh worked for a Sindhi firm in Singapore. The firm imported clothes from Malaysia, China and other places in the East, and Suresh, who had left for Singapore from Bombay at the age of fifteen, did mostly door-to-door sales. Seven years into his employment, Suresh felt the call of 'the freedom to do what he wanted'. Word got around among Sindhis that business was taking off in Liberia, and in 1963, the whole family moved there. During their first year there,

Suresh bought textiles and clothes locally and sold them on to retailers. He then took the step of importing textiles directly, mostly from Thailand and the Philippines, and he did this from 1963 to 1971, when he changed tack to selling stationery and office equipment. There was much less competition in that line and it was a wise move. The business thrived and, over time, Suresh recruited a number of Sindhis from India to work for him. At least eight of them eventually started their own businesses and are now his direct competitors in the stationery trade. Arun remembers that the 1970s were 'brilliant times' to be doing business in Liberia, not least since it was a relatively safe environment. What happened in the 1980s and 1990s is well known, and the business of the Moolchandanis and of thousands of other Sindhis was seriously disrupted, to the extent that many of them left the country altogether. From 1968 to 1973, Arun was sent to a boarding school in Buckinghamshire, where he was the only Indian pupil. The school had been recommended by Arun's paternal uncle, who lived in Surrey and who was in business exporting to Liberia to his brother, Suresh. Arun's holidays were spent with his family in Liberia. As it turned out, Arun ended up settling permanently in the UK. Even while still in secondary school, he helped out with his uncle's business. It was a productive time, for he was taught the export trade and the brass tacks of daily business deals. In 1980, at twenty, Arun was set up by his father (who provided capital and a 'director' in whose name the new

firm was registered) as the main supplier to the family
business in Liberia. His own supplies of stationery
came mainly from producers in the UK and Brazil,
but he was also supplied US-made goods through
a cousin on his mother's side. In Liberia, his clients
included local banks, businesses and UN peacekeeping
forces.

Suresh Kirpalani

Suresh Kirpalani owns and runs a four-star hotel in
Mumbai. He comes from a bhaiband family, originally
from Tando Adam in Sindh, where the main family
business was cotton gins. (His family were not
Sindhworkis.) Suresh prides himself on the extent and
unity of his bradari. He cites the example of his father,
who moved to Dubai in 1954 and within a few years
managed to get around fifty cousins to move there.
Many of them still operate in Dubai, and there are other
bradari members in Spain, London, east Africa, the
US and in several cities in India. They are particularly
well connected in India, in fact, and regularly meet at
weddings and other events. Back to Suresh's father . . .
he first moved to India, 'penniless', in 1948. He and
his brothers looked for jobs here and there—'any jobs,
because beggars can't be choosers'. They moved first
to Ajmer, then to Calcutta, where they opened a small
tea stall. In 1950, they settled in Ulhasnagar. Suresh's
father found a job with a Sindhwork firm in Bombay
and commuted daily to and from the city. His break
came in 1954, when the firm sent him on a business

trip to Dubai. There, he happened to come across a Sindhwork firm of substantial business clout. But the firm was in the process of winding down its operations in Dubai ('it was a difficult place to live in at the time, there was little infrastructure'). It was in fact one of the directors of the firm, who was in Dubai to close down the business, that Suresh's father ran into. Seeing the chance of a lifetime, he offered to run the Dubai branch for the firm, hardship or no hardship. It must have been a convincing bid, because he got the job and slowly rebuilt the firm's operations, at one point employing up to 250 people, of whom around half were Sindhi. It was at this firm that Suresh, then a young man, started his career. He is a qualified engineer, and his first job was at a factory the firm owned in Nigeria, where he spent fourteen months. This was followed by eleven months at a textile factory the firm owned in Indonesia. Suresh then left the firm and moved to India, where he got married. Together with his father, he decided to use his savings to set up his own business. It had always been his father's wish for the family to have a firm business base in India, which was now 'their country'. 'After fifty years in Dubai, my father still does not hold a UAE passport. Things are now fairly good, but you never know.' They set up a small import and export business in Mumbai, and after some years managed to put together enough capital to buy a small hotel. It has since been refurbished and upgraded, and there are now advanced plans to buy a small hotel, which they refurbished and upgraded. Suresh tells me that a substantial number of Sindhis in Mumbai are in the hotel business, and that Sindhis from around the world who visit Mumbai often stay at places owned by or run by family or people known to them.

Manish Bharwani

Manish Bharwani's family originally came from Karachi. In 1947, and still in his early twenties, Manish's father left for Uganda, where his sister, who had married into a family in business there, lived. They were based in Jinja, which at the time was little more than a village. There were three Sindhi families there, all in business, and the Bharwanis ran a small shop that sold all manner of goods. The reason why three Sindhi families ended up in a village in Uganda was the presence of large numbers of Sikh, Gujarati, and other Indians there— and thus a good market—owing to major infrastructural works happening in the region. In 1949, they moved to Kampala and opened a larger store, the Sindh General Store, stocked largely through suppliers in the UK and manned by Gujarati and Ismaili shop assistants. This was a step up in the world, since Kampala was a commercial hub with a marked British presence and a demand for quality goods. Manish himself was born in Kampala in 1952. In 1961, his father died young and his mother ceded his share of the business to her in-laws and took up a job as a teacher. She resolved that her children would not become shopkeepers. She would, however, still sometimes help out at the shop, where she would be joined by Manish and his brother Surej. In 1968, at sixteen, Manish left for London to study.

This was a time when serious trouble was brewing for Indians in Uganda (Idi Amin came to power in 1971). The Bharwani family business and thousands of other Indian businesses in the country were being dismantled. Manish's mother managed to liquidate some of her property and transfer some of her assets to the UK. Manish's brother Surej moved to Algiers, where his maternal uncles had worked for the Sindhworki firm Pohumull and eventually set up their own small businesses. After Algiers, Surej moved to Paris, where he opened a shop, and eventually to Taipei to join his in-laws' business (he had met and got married to a Sindhi while on a visit to London). Apparently, the Bharwanis were in fact, the first Sindhis in Taipei. It was not to be Surej's last move: in the early 1980s, he moved to London to be with his brother Manish, who had meanwhile met and got married to a Sindhi from Tenerife. It was around this time that Manish, who was well-qualified, got a job with a major Sindhwork firm which had offices around the world, including in London. He has never quite felt the compulsion to set up on his own, and for several years occupied a high-ranking and well-paid post with the firm. It helped that the owners of the firm, with whom he is on a first-name basis, were 'excellent' employers.

Sabu Rupani

The biography of Sabu Rupani is telling. He was born into an old amil family in the Hirabad neighbourhood of Hyderabad in 1923. The family was part of a select circle of well-educated amils who had close and long-standing associations with the British and the public services. They were looked up to by bhaibands, as well as by amil families of lesser standing. Sabu's grandfather was a railway officer, his father a forestry officer, and his three paternal uncles a doctor, a teacher and a zamindar each. In Hyderabad, he attended D.G. National College, which had been set up in 1922, partly with the help of British theosophist and activist Dr Annie Besant. (After Partition, it became and still is R.D. National College in Bombay.) He then studied in Karachi, and in 1943 graduated with a BSc degree in physics and chemistry. There was little industry in Sindh at the time, and he joined the American Air Force in a middle-management office job. Sabu never considered a Sindhwork job—as he put it, this was an option for bhaiband 'boys' who were not well educated and who had to endure all manner of exploitation by their employers. After a year and a half with the air force, Sabu moved to British Overseas Airways Corporation (BOAC), where he worked in store management in Karachi. In 1947, his family left Sindh and moved to Ahmedabad. Sabu tried, but did not manage to get himself transferred to BOAC's office in India, and in 1948 he left Sindh for Bombay. There, a distant relative of his on his mother's side brought together eight people to invest in a battery manufacturing business. Sabu's share, which was Rs 25,000, was provided to him by his father. The firm, which at one point employed about eighty people (Maharashtrians, mostly), went bankrupt after four years of wobbly operations. All but penniless at this point, Sabu decided to try his luck in the UK. He arrived in London in 1953 with a total of £120 in his pocket, and rented a room in South Kensington for £3 a week. A few unproductive weeks later, he got a job at a battery engineering company in Ilford. He worked there for seventeen years. During this time, he raised a family (he married a Sindhi woman in 1958) and purchased a family home in Ilford in 1963. At one point, two of his Sindhi friends in London were working with a Sindhi trading firm. The owner was known for treating his employees well and giving them good salaries. The firm's business was the import of flour, sugar and other commodities from Brazil and their re-export to Nigeria. Financial and other reasons made Sabu reconsider his vow to never work for a Sindhi company, and when he was offered a job at a confirming house in 1970, he took it. Sabu did not really know the owner, but during the interview much was made of his family connections back in Hyderabad. The business involved the financing and brokerage of trade between Sindhi suppliers in the Far East and Sindhi importers in west Africa. Sabu worked for the confirming house for four years, until it ran into problems. Pressured by bad circumstances and the taxman, Sindhi importers in Nigeria temporarily shut down business. The confirming house in London found itself cash-strapped, and it was only after Sabu was sent to Nigeria to try to negotiate some kind of settlement that the company avoided total bankruptcy. Sabu was not particularly rewarded for his efforts and felt short-changed, but there was a twist to this tale. On his last night in Nigeria, he meant a Sindhi couple in Lagos who told him that their business was at a low ebb and that they could do with a good manager for their ailing confirming house in London. Sabu saw his chance, and since 1974, he has worked with a total of eight Sindhi companies as their branch manager in London. His last job before his retirement in 1989 was with a Sindhi real estate business in London.

Jagdish Balani

The Rug Gallery is a wholesale rug business which operates from a large warehouse in North London. It was established in 1983 by Jagdish Balani, whose family was originally from Khairpur District but had moved to Larkana. It was a bania family of modest means. In 1947, the family left Sindh by train for Bombay. Jagdish grew up in Bombay, where he attended a Maharashtrian school and later Sitaram Prakash High School. While in the seventh grade, his elder brother (who had worked various odd jobs in Bombay since before Partition) found him a place at Robert Money Technical High School, where English was the language of instruction and engineering held pride of place. Jagdish found it hard to cope and was soon moved to a school where Sindhi was more regularly spoken. After his matriculation, he enrolled in a college of commerce in the Churchgate area of Mumbai and graduated with success. The job offers that followed included one from his brother, who asked him to join his small fruit vending business, and another from K. Chellaram, who offered him a job in Nigeria. Neither appeared too attractive to Jagdish, who instead joined the Life Insurance Corporation of India as an insurance salesman. The task proved harder than he thought, and he decided to join his brother after all. It did not take him long to realize that shopkeeping was not going to be his gateway to riches. In 1965, alone and with not much to his name, he left for the UK. His first job was in packaging, in the ceramics department at Harrods. In his spare time, he also managed to make Sindhi friends and socialize with them. Predictably, someone suggested he work for K. Chellaram. He took up a job in the shipping department, which at the time employed sixteen (of whom seven were Sindhis) at its London offices in the city. Conditions were good, but the pay was not, and six months into his Chellaram job Jagdish took up an offer from a carpet business run by a Jewish family. On the side, he took to setting up and running a stall on the weekends in Petticoat Lane or the market in Oxford. His line was cheap electronic goods, which he would source on generous credit terms from Sindhi suppliers in London. His ambition to make money never left him, and in 1977 he started a little of his own business in rugs. He was eventually approached by a Punjabi friend of his who was looking for a UK importer for his new carpet export business in India. Jagdish had no capital, but the terms were good and they started importing from India. In 1983, Jagdish separated amicably from his Punjabi partner and set up on his own, importing carpets from several parts of Asia as well as Romania.

Gope Lalwani

Gope Lalwani was born into a bhaiband family in Hyderabad in 1933. His great-grandfather had been a trader in Aden, and the plan was for his grandfather, Lal, to follow him. When he was still a boy, however, Lal had a big quarrel with his stepmother and ran away from home. He had helped himself to a handful of coins as he left the house, and he used them to buy and sell little things. When he returned home with his coins and a profit, his father blessed him and told him that 'life would smile upon him'. Some time after this incident, Lal left Sindh to trade, usually from bumboats, in Bombay and Zanzibar. He did well enough to make it to Mozambique, where he was eventually joined by his brother from Aden. By the time he died in 1936, the business had footholds in a number of places in east Africa. By this time the two brothers ran the business with their sons, and it was decided to split the operation. Gope's father, Ram, got the part that was into importing curios and other wares from India and Japan and selling them in east Africa, where the shops had names like 'Bombay Bazaar' and 'Casa Choitram' (in Portuguese). They had a good number of employees, all of whom were Sindhi bhaibands on formal job contracts (the contract documents doubled as travel and residence permits). In 1947, the whole family left Sindh for Bombay, where they had a business office. From there they moved on to East Africa, where their shops were located. Many of their employees did the same, and brought over their families from Sindh. Before Partition, the system had been for the firm to provide its employees (men, exclusively) with living quarters; now the employees had families and found housing of their own. In many cases they went their separate ways with respect to business, too. Gope remembers a great-uncle who worked for the family firm, and who disagreed with the firm's decision to close down a shop they had in South Africa. He left the firm and set up a clothing business in South Africa, doing so well that Gope's father, his former employer, eventually started to import goods from him. Partition, and the relocation and reorganization of families that resulted, seems to have been a particularly busy time for employees of Sindhwork firms to set up their own small businesses. Gope's own childhood spanned three places: Hyderabad, Bombay and Nairobi. In Nairobi, as a teenager, he would help run his father's shop. When he left school, it was a natural progression into the family business, where he worked for a number of years. That was until politics got in the way of business and personal security in the early 1970s. Gope remembers that it was becoming impossible to trade. Inspectors would raid the premises and clamp down on him for 'hoarding', for the intriguing reason that most of the stock was kept in warehouses rather than on display. Gope, like many other Sindhis in Nairobi, held a British passport. And, like many others, he moved to the UK, partly because of the impossible business conditions in Africa but also in search of better education prospects for his children. At first, he would divide his time between London and Nairobi, but in 1980 he moved to the UK permanently. His first business was 'Pound Saver', a hardware store. Some years later he opened a general import-export business with his brother. Given the good contacts they had around the world—a legacy of their years of trade in Africa—they found it relatively easy to establish themselves in business in the UK.

EPILOGUE

We have no way of knowing what Seth Naomul would make of twenty-first-century Indonesian soap operas. Five thousand kilometres is a long distance, and between Karachi and Jakarta lie 200 years of tricky terrain too. He might say that his truth was stranger than the fiction of the operas, but that is pure guesswork on my part. We would be on a surer footing to say that he would recognize his descendants and their ways of working.

Scholar and specialist on Indonesia Maria Myutel has documented a contemporary and fascinating case which is well worth taking up in some detail.[1] There are 8,000 to 10,000 Sindhis settled in Indonesia today. Most of them live in Jakarta and are known generically as '*orang India*' ('Indian people'). As we have seen, Sindhworkis had been trading in the region for decades, but it was in the late 1940s and early 1950s that the Partition exodus brought in whole families from Sindh. In 1949, the Bombay Merchants Association was set up in Indonesia, and it defined its membership in no unclear terms: 'BMA is exclusively for people of

Sindhi descent, not anyone else.' At around the same time, the Gandhi Memorial School was established in the country to serve the needs of Sindhi children. The large majority of Sindhis in Indonesia today are in business, typically in the textiles trade, but there is a twist to this tale.

Starting in the 1950s, a growing number of Sindhis cast their eyes on a chance that would make them quite unique outside of India: they entered and shaped the media industries—first cinema and later, from the 1990s, national television. Typically, it all started with trade. Already, in the first few years following Partition, a number of Sindhis in Indonesia were importing, distributing and screening Indian and American films. This made them familiar with both local commercial practices and international distribution networks. It was on these foundations that they rose to considerable prominence as producers of local titles. In the 1970s and 1980s, up to a quarter of the annual film production in Indonesia was in the hands of Sindhis.

Then, in the late 1980s, Indonesia liberalized television in an attempt to retain audiences, at a time when new technologies were chipping away at state control. There was a sudden surge in demand for content, which was met by foreign production imported for the most part by Sindhi traders, to which there was some resistance by the moralists in Indonesia, who railed against what they saw as the corruption of indigenous Indonesian values. More importantly, the stage was set for independent production, and the Sindhis stepped in to develop a new and lucrative industry sector—production of *sinetron* (soap opera). There were many reasons why they were well placed to do so. They had access to sources of capital, for one, and they also could draw on three decades of experience in the film industry, as we have seen. The former proved especially pivotal. The main problem faced by aspiring producers at the time was access to funds. Local banks were extremely reluctant to finance what they deemed to be a risky and volatile sector. Sindhis, however, could tap into their community resources. At least three Indonesian banks—Bank Swadesi, Bank Rama and Bank Subendra—were part-owned by prominent Sindhi business families. What's more, the fact that Sindhi producers usually ran side businesses stood them in good stead with the banks, which reckoned there were better chances of recovery from other sources in the event of flops. Finally, Sindhis could also draw (often in the form of personal loans, in cash) on the capital that circulated within the global Sindhi community.

Finance aside, Sindhis were also in a strong position to import labour from the US, India and elsewhere to bridge the 'creativity gap'—the endemic shortage of specialized labour, that is—which hindered the local film and sinetron market. Through their connections in Bollywood, Sindhi producers found it relatively easy to import Indian actors, production teams and other personnel who were affordable, experienced, spoke English and Hindi, and learned Indonesian quickly. But the potential of Sindhi locals was not overlooked either. The Sindhi-owned studios were managed by

hard-nosed Sindhi businesspeople from Indonesia hired
especially for the job. They had a granular understanding
of local audiences, tastes and markets—skills that proved
particularly fruitful in the production of sinetron. So
successful was the model, and so marked was the effect on
artistic autonomy of keeping business within the family,
so to say, that Sindhi producers actually came up with
an innovative product, *sinetron Ramadhan*, which in turn
evolved into a new genre of Indonesian television shows
known as *sinetron Islam* (Islamic soap opera). It would
be wrong to say that the Indonesian media industry was
simply a door left ajar, which Sindhis slipped through
in search of easy profits. They may have done that, but
they also reshaped Indonesian cinema, and especially
television, in fundamental ways. Making a quick buck
and enterprise and innovation are two separate species of
activity, so to say, and certainly in this case, the Sindhis
were in the latter camp.

I said in the beginning of this book that there is no
such thing as a Sindhi miracle. I have not changed my
mind, but I do find it staggering to be able to recognize,
in such a specific example as Indonesian soap opera, so
many of the community traits that have been the leit
motifs of Sindhi *artha* for such a long time. The story
of Sindhi business cannot provide fixed formulas on
how to be successful at doing business. In the process
of charting our economic future, however, it is good to
think with.

GLOSSARY

amil: a Hindu Sindhi jati whose members were historically associated with administrative and public service roles in Sindh, especially under the Talpur Mirs and during the British period.

Bahrano Sahib: a ritual composite intended to represent Jhulelal, involving food and a procession.

bania: a generic word for 'trader'.

bhaiband: literally 'brotherhood', a Hindu Sindhi jati whose members were and are associated with trade and business historically, notably with Sindhwork.

bradari: among Sindhis, mostly used to mean an extended kin group.

Cheti Chand: the first new moon of the year, associated with Jhulelal and commonly celebrated as the Sindhi New Year.

gumashta: an agent.

hundi: a financial instrument used by indigenous bankers and traders, usually a promissory note.

lohana: a jati historically associated with the north-western regions of the subcontinent, and which subsumes a large number of regional and occupational sub-types.

Nanakpanth: a follower of Guru Nanak, the first of the ten Sikh Gurus.

pedhi: a shop or seat of an office from where business is conducted.

pir: a Muslim saint or holy man.

Sindhwork: a type of trade which arose in the mid-nineteenth century, and which originally involved trade in the regional crafts of Sindh ('Sindh works') by highly mobile traders known as 'Sindhworkis'.

shroff: a moneylender/indigenous banker.

tikana: a mandir which usually includes both the Sikh Guru Granth Sahib and images of Hindu deities.

wadero: a Sindhi large landholder.

zamindar: a landowner.

NOTES

1. Who Are the Sindhis?

1   Population Census 2017, Pakistan Bureau of Statistics, Government of Pakistan.

2   Census of India, 1901.

3   Salazar, *Momentous Mobilities*.

4   Kothari, *The Persistence of Partitions*.

5   Asrani, *Doing Business the Shikarpuri-Sindhi Way'*, p. 274.

2. Beginnings

1   Hotchand, *A Forgotten Chapter of Indian History*.

2   Ahmad, *India and the Neighbouring Territories*, pp. 40–45.

3   Jhangiani, *Shah Abdul Latif*, pp. 131–53.

4   Floor, *The Dutch East India Company*.

5   Cheesman, 'Local power and colonial authority'; Cheesman, *'Power in Rural Sind'*.

6   See for instance the 'Replies to Revenue queries by the Collectors of Hyderabad, Shikarpoor, and Kurrachee, 28 September 1843' in *Reports & c on the Administration of Scinde, Accounts and Papers*, 1854.

7   Cheesman, *The Omnipresent Bania*.

8   Pottinger, *Travels in Beloochistan and Sinde*.

9   Postans, *Personal observations on Sindh*.

10 Markovits, *The Global World of Indian Merchants*. The section on Shikarpuri trade in Central Asia and elsewhere in the nineteenth century is based primarily on this excellent source.

11 McMurdo, 'An account of the country of Sindh'.

12 As cited in Markovits, op. cit., p. 57.

13 'Letter from the Political Agent for the Affairs of Sinde to the Secretary to the Government of India', *Correspondence Relative to Sinde, 1836–1843*.

14 Letter from Tarachand, a merchant in the Sudder Bazaar at Sukkur, to the Assistant Police Agent at Sukkur (1841?); and Petition from Kotamul to Lieutenant Brown (30 July, 1842), *Correspondence Relative to Sinde, 1836-1843*.

15 Burton, *Sind Revisited*.

16 McMurdo, op. cit.

3. The Sindhworkis of Hyderabad

1   Burnes, *A narrative of a visit to the court of Sinde*.

2   'Catalogue of Scinde Prize Booty for sale in Bombay on the 1ˢᵗ of March, 1846'.

3   Askari & Crill, *Colours of the Indus*.

4   Pottinger, *Travels in Beloochistan and Sinde*.

5   Burnes, op. cit.

6   'Replies to Revenue Queries by the Collectors of Hyderabad, Shikarpoor, and Kurrachee, 28 September 1843,' in *Reports & c. on the Administration of Scinde*, 1854.

7 Baillie, *Sind*; Choksey, *The Story of Sind*; Hughes, *A Gazetteer of the Province of Sindh*.

8 *Annual Statement of the Trade and Navigation of the Province of Sind, 1870–1, 1890–1.*

9 'The Gazetteer of Bombay City and Island', 1909.

10 Chugani, *Indians in Japan*.

11 Mahtani, *Origins of the Indian Community in Ghana*.

12 Chattopadhyaya, *Indians in Sri Lanka*.

13 Merani & van der Laan, *The Indian traders in Sierra Leone*.

14 White, *Turbans & Traders*, p. 5.

15 Markovits, *The Global World of Indian Merchants*.

16 Haller, 'Place and ethnicity in two merchant diasporas', p. 81.

17 Tindall, *City of Gold*.

18 Petition to the Chief Secretary of Government 4949/1887, National Archives Malta.

19 Petition to the Chief Secretary of Government 1466/1916, National Archives Malta.

20 Petition to the Chief Secretary of Government 726/1919, 2486/1916, 1499/1919, 698/1920, National Archives Malta.

21 Markovits, op. cit.

22 Daswani, *Kishinchand Chellaram*, p. 43.

23 Markovits, op. cit., 132–33.

24 Ross, *The Land of the Five Rivers and Sindh*.

25 Sorley, *Shah Abdul Latif of Bhit*, p. 42.

26 Postans, *Personal observations on Sindh*, p. 102.

27 Hughes, op. cit.

28 Ross, op. cit.

29 Tillotson, *The Tradition of Indian Architecture*.

30 Chugani, op. cit.

31   Chattopadhyaya, op. cit.

32   Merani & van der Laan, op. cit.

33   Daswani, op. cit.

34   Chugani, op. cit.

35   Merani & van der Laan, op cit.

36   Daswani, op. cit., 51.

37   Banks, 'Why Move?'.

38   Petition to the Chief Secretary of Government 1822/1906, National Archives Malta.

4. An Enduring Legacy

1   Haller, 'Place and Ethnicity in Two Merchant Diasporas'.

2   Vaid, *The Overseas Indian Community in Hong Kong*, p. 92.

3   Markovits, *The Global World of Indian Merchants 1750-1947*, p. 284.

4   White, *Turbans and Traders*, p. 184.

5   Xavier & Gomez, 'Still an ethnic enterprise after a generational change?'.

5. Sindhi Business in India after Partition

1   Kothari, *The Persistence of Partitions*, p. 389.

2   Markovits, *The Global World of Indian Merchants 1750-1947*.

3   'Report of the Indian Central Banking Enquiry Committee', Government of India, 1931, p. 73.

4   'The Reserve Bank of India Banking Commission Report', 1972, p 10.

5 Vakil & Cabinetmaker, *Government and the Displaced Persons*.
6 Alexander, *New Citizens of India*, p. 65.
7 Barnouw, 'The Social Structure of a Sindhi Refugee Community'.
8 Vakil & Cabinetmaker, op. cit., p. 5.
9 Karunakaran, *Ulhasnagar*.
10 'Report of the Ownership Flats Enquiry Committee', Government of Maharashtra, 1962.
11 Barnouw, op. cit., pp. 150–51.
12 Dhabhai, *The Purusharthi Refugee*, p. 3.
13 Dhabhai, op. cit., p. 2.

6. The Culture of Business

1 Haller, 'Place and ethnicity in two merchant diasporas'.
2 Swayne-Thomas, *Indian Summer*, p. 10.
3 Ward, 'Worth its weight', p. 94.
4 Ward, op. cit., p. 3.

7. Biographies of Unknown Sindhis

1 Chaudhuri, *The Autobiography of an Unknown Indian*.

Epilogue

1 Myutel, 'Commercial television in Indonesia'.

BIBLIOGRAPHY

S.M. Ahmad, *India and the Neighbouring Territories in the Kitab Nuzhat Al-Mushtaq Fi' Khtiraq Al-'Afaq of Al-Sharid Al-Idrisi,* Leiden: E.J. Brill, 1960.

H. Alexander, *New Citizens of India,* Oxford University Press: London & Toronto, 1951.

N. Askari & R. Crill, *Colours of the Indus: Costume and textiles of Pakistan,* Merrell Holberton and the Victorian and Albert Museum, London, 1997.

N. Asrani, 'Doing business, the Shikarpuri-Sindhi way', *Sindhi Tapestry: An anthology of reflections on the Sindhi identity*, S S Aggarwal (ed.), Black-And-White Fountain, Pune, 2020, pp. 267-74.

A.F. Baillie, *India, Ceylon, Straits Settlements, British North Borneo, Hong Kong,* Kegan Paul, Trench, Trübner, London, 1899.

M. Banks, 'Why Move? Regional and long distance migrations of Gujarati Jains', *Migration: The Asian experience*, eds. J.M. Brown and R. Foot, St Martin's Press and St Anthony's College, Oxford, 1994, pp. 131–48.

V. Barnouw, 'The social structure of a Sindhi refugee community', *Social Forces,* 33 (2), 1954, pp. 142–52.

J. Burnes, *A narrative of a visit to the court of Sinde,* Robert Cadell, Edinburgh, 1831.

R.F. Burton, *Sind Revisited: With Notices of the Anglo-Indian Army; Railroads; Past, Present, and Future, etc*. (2 Vols), Richard Bentley and Son, London, 1877.

H. Chattopadhyaya, *Indians in Sri Lanka: A historical study,* OPS Publishers Private Ltd, Calcutta, 1979.

N.C. Chaudhuri, *The Autobiography of an Unknown Indian*, Macmillan, London, 1951.

D. Cheesman, 'Local Power and Colonial Authority: The Pax Britannica in 19th Century Sind', *History Today*, 1981a, pp. 23–26.

D. Cheesman, 'Power in Rural Sind in the late Nineteenth Century', *Asian Affairs*, XII (I), 1981b, pp. 57–67.

D. Cheesman, 'The Omnipresent Bania: Rural Moneylenders in Nineteenth-Century Sind', *Modern Asian Studies*, 16 (3), 1982, pp. 445–62.

R.D. Choksey, *The Story of Sind (An Economic Survey) 1843-1933,* Dastane Ramchandra, Pune, 1983.

A.G. Chugani, 'Indians in Japan: A case study of the Sindhis in Kobe', Unpublished MA dissertation submitted to the University of Hawaii, 1982.

K. Daswani, *Kishinchand Chellaram: Sindhi pathfinder,* Linda Watkins & Associates, Hong Kong, 1998.

G. Dhabhai, 'The Purusharthi Refugee: Sindhi migrants in Jaipur's walled city', *Economic & Political Weekly* 53 (4), 2018, pp. 1–11.

W. Floor, *The Dutch East India Company (VOC) and Diewel-Sind (Pakistan) in the 17th and 18th centuries,* University of Karachi, Karachi, 1993–94.

D. Haller, 'Place and ethnicity in two merchant diasporas: A comparison of Sindhis and Jews in Gibraltar', *Global Networks* 3 (1), 2003, pp. 75–96.

Seth Naomul Hotchand, *A Forgotten Chapter of Indian History as described in the Memoirs of Seth Naomi Hotchand, C.S.I., of Karachi 1804-1878,* (Written in Sindhi in 1871, translated by Rao Bahadur Alumal Trikamdas Bhojwani, edited and with an introduction by H. Evans, M. James), William Pollard, Exeter, 1915.

A.W. Hughes, *A Gazetteer of the Province of Sindh,* George Bell, London, 1874.

S.M. Jhangiani, *Shah Abdul Latif and his Times (1690 AD to 1751 AD)*, University of Delhi, Delhi, 1987.

T.K. Karunakaran, 1958. 'Ulhasnagar: A sociological study in urban development', Unpublished MA dissertation submitted to the Department of Sociology, University of Bombay, 1987.

R. Kothari, 'The Persistence of Partitions: A study of the Sindhi Hindus in India', *Interventions* 13 (3), 2011, pp. 386–97.

P. Mahtani, 'Origins of the Indian Community in Ghana', *BR International,* 34 (12), 1997, pp. 14–16.

C. Markovits, *The Global World of Indian Merchants 1750-1947: Traders of Sind from Bukhara to Panama*, Cambridge University Press, Cambridge, 2000.

Captain J. McMurdo, 'An Account of the Country of Sindh; with Remarks on the State of Society, the Government, Manners, and Customs of the People', *The Journal of the Royal Asiatic Society of Great Britain and Ireland* 1, 1834 [1812–1814], pp. 223-257.

H.V. Merani & H.L. van der Laan, 'The Indian Traders in Sierra Leone', *African Affairs,* 78, 1979, pp. 240–50.

M. Myutel, 'Commercial television in Indonesia: The Sindhi element', *Bijdragen tot de Taal- Land- en Volkenkunde,* 175 (2/3), 2019, pp. 155–76.

T. Postans, *Personal Observations on Sindh; The Manners and Customs of its inhabitants; and its productive capabilities: with a sketch of its history, a narrative of recent events, and an account of the connection of the British Government with that country to the present period*, Longman, Brown, Green and Longmans, London, 1843.

H. Pottinger, *Travels in Beloochistan and Sinde: Accompanied by a geographical and historical account of those countries, with a map*, Longman, Hurst, Rees, Orme and Brown, London, 1816.

D. Ross, *The Land of the Five Rivers and Sindh,* Chapman and Hall, London, 1883.

N.B. Salazar, *Momentous Mobilities: Anthropological musings on the meanings of travel,* Berghahn, New York & Oxford, 2018.

H.T. Sorley, *Shah Abdul Latif of Bhit: His poetry, life and times,* Oxford University Press, Pakistan, 1940.

A. Swayne-Thomas, *Indian Summer: A Mem-sahib in India and Sind,* New English Library, London, 1981.

G.H.R. Tillotson, *The tradition of Indian architecture: Continuity, controversy and change since 1850,* Yale University Press, London, 1989.

G. Tindall, *City of Gold: The biography of Bombay,* Temple Smith, London, 1982.

K.N. Vaid, *The Overseas Indian Community in Hong Kong,* University of Hong Kong, Hong Kong, 1972.

C.N. Vakil & P.H. Cabinetmaker, *Government and the Displaced Persons: A study in social tensions,* Vora, Bombay, 1956.

H. Ward, 'Worth its Weight: Gold, Women and Value in North West India', Unpublished Ph.D. Thesis submitted to the Department of Social Anthropology, University of Cambridge, 1997.

B.S. White, *Turbans and Traders: Hong Kong's Indian communities,* Oxford University Press, Hong Kong, 1994.

J.A. Xavier & E.T. Gomez, 'Still an ethnic enterprise after a generational change? Indian-owned SMEs in Malaysia', *Journal of southeast Asian Studies,* 49 (2), 2018, pp. 297–322.